GW00566733

King Henry

King Henry

Henry Shefflin
Irish Sporting Legend

Paul O'Flynn

Gill Books

Gill Books
Hume Avenue
Park West
Dublin 12
www.gillbooks.ie

Gill Books is an imprint of M.H. Gill & Co.

978 07171 9082 9

Edited by Jane Rogers
Proofread by Sally Vince

Printed by ScandBook, Sweden
This book is typeset in 12 on 18pt Tahoma.

The paper used in this book comes from the wood pulp of managed forests. For every tree felled, at least one tree is planted, thereby renewing natural resources.

This book has been produced in accordance with guidelines provided by The Dyslexia Association of Ireland.

A CIP catalogue record for this book is available from the British Library.

5 4 3 2 1

Author's Note

This book is based on Henry Shefflin's life and career. It would be impossible for me to go back in time and listen in to all of the conversations with Henry that have taken place over the years, so I have had to imagine them. I also haven't actually been in the dressing rooms or Henry's home or inside his head, because that would just be weird. However, all of the scores and matches are real and all of Henry's achievements mentioned in the book are factual. He really is one of the greatest hurlers ever.

About the Author

Paul O'Flynn is an RTÉ News and Sport presenter and journalist. A graduate of DCU, with a BA in Journalism and an MA in International Relations, he is also an associate lecturer at his alma mater. He is a keen sportsperson and amateur swimmer, and in 2018 he was the winner of the Liffey Swim.

Chapter 1

Penalty King

The skies were dark and the rain was falling. But the weather didn't matter to Henry. Not today. Today the only thing on his mind was winning the All-Ireland. The biggest prize in hurling. He looked out of the window at the hundreds of fans lining the streets as the team bus snaked its way towards Croke Park. They were dressed in the blue and yellow of Tipperary or the black and amber stripes of Henry's team, Kilkenny. Their faces were painted, they were cheering, waving and hooting horns. Henry looked around at his teammates in silence, taking it all in. It wasn't a time for talk. Henry had been here before, plenty of times. On a good day, Croke Park was his favourite place on earth. But on a bad day there was nowhere worse. He took a deep breath as the bus drove through the gates and under the tunnel right into the heart of the great stadium. Henry stepped off the bus to the flash of cameras as he made his way to the dressing room. This was it. Showtime.

Over the years Henry had far more good days than bad in Croke Park. He was widely known as the greatest hurler who ever played the game, the star player on the best team ever to step onto a hurling pitch. Kilkenny had won the last three All-Irelands and nobody could touch them. The Cats, as they were known, were unstoppable. But right now, Henry was nervous. He didn't feel right. It wasn't like the other years. He was feeling the pressure because Kilkenny had a chance to create history by winning four All-Irelands in a row. Something only one other team had done in more than 100 years. Standing in the way were Tipperary, playing their first All-Ireland final in eight years. They were a young team full of talent, like Eoin Kelly, Lar Corbett and Seamie Callanan. They had pushed Kilkenny all the way in the league final earlier that year. They were hungry for success.

Henry knew all about Tipperary and how good they were. But he wasn't afraid. Why should he be? Kilkenny had stars of their own. Not just Henry but Eoin Larkin, Eddie Brennan and Richie Hogan too. And they had the best manager in the game. The great Brian Cody. A tough man who knew everything there was to know about the game of hurling. A born winner and a genius at training teams to win All-Irelands.

Henry fiddled with the straps of his helmet, tightening them just a little. He tapped his hurl a couple of times on the dressing-room floor. He knew the routine of All-Ireland final day.

But he couldn't shake the nerves. His tummy was twisted in knots. 'Come on, Henry!' he said to himself. 'What's wrong with you?' He tied his bootlaces and jumped to his feet, shaking his legs a little to loosen them out. He looked around the dressing room at the other players. They weren't just his teammates. They were friends. Brothers. They shared a special bond. A love of hurling and, more important, a love of winning.

The referee knocked on the door. It was time. Almost half-past three on the first Sunday of September. 'Come on, lads!' roared Brian Cody, slapping each player on the back as they charged towards the tunnel. He saved a special word for Henry as he whizzed past. 'We'll do it today, Henry,' he whispered. 'Have no doubts.'

Henry felt 10 feet tall. That's all it ever took from Cody. A quiet word to put your mind at ease. Henry puffed out his chest as they stood in the tunnel. The noise of the crowd was deafening. More than 82,000 screaming fans. The black and amber half hoping for history.

The blue and yellow with other ideas.

The national anthem played and then the referee took the ball in his hand and put the whistle to his lips. Henry casually clipped on the straps of his green helmet and tightened his grip on his hurl. Game on!

Tipp started like a flash, running like their lives depended on it. But Kilkenny got the first score. A handy free in. The best way for Henry to calm his nerves. He lined up the free. He stared at the posts, looked to the sliotar and back up to the posts again. His routine was like clockwork and he hardly ever missed. He rolled the ball onto the base of the hurl, rose it into the air and swung with precision. The ball, as ever, flew straight between the posts. Kilkenny were in front and Henry was off the mark.

The match was hectic right from the start. Both teams charged into each other and traded score for score. The clashes were ferocious. Kilkenny had to work so hard for every score. Everyone knew straightaway it would be a classic.

At half-time Kilkenny were just ahead, 13 points to 11. Henry had scored five of their points. But the drama was only starting.

Tipp burst into life again in the second half. Henry watched in disbelief as Seamie Callanan charged in on goal and let rip. The sliotar looked to be flying into the back of the net. But Kilkenny's goalkeeper, PJ Ryan, had other ideas.

What a save!

Minutes later PJ did it again. This time from an Eoin Kelly shot.

Unbelievable! PJ Ryan! How did he keep it out?

Henry had a sinking feeling. He wasn't playing at his best and Kilkenny were in trouble.

'Come on, lads!' he roared. 'We can't keep relying on PJ to make all the saves!'

Fired up now, Henry grabbed another two points and with 15 minutes to go the sides were level.

Then Tipp pulled away again. Three quick-fire points left the Cats reeling. Their dream of four in a row was slipping away. Henry knew he had to do something special. Luckily the referee helped him out.

Penalty!

Richie Power was stopped as he ran towards goal. It looked a soft one. But Henry didn't care. This was the chance he needed.

He stepped forward and placed the sliotar on the line. The great goalkeeper Brendan Cummins stood in his way, along with Pádraic Maher and Conor O'Mahony. Henry didn't wait too long. He picked his spot early, took a breath and blocked out the noise of the crowd. This was it. One shot at glory. The All-Ireland final, the historic four in a row, a place in history all came down to this one puck. He imagined he was a young boy again, playing for fun in the field at home, practising on his own with nobody watching. He lifted the ball and smashed a sizzling shot right into the spot he had picked. Cummins stretched out his hurl and got the slightest touch. But it wasn't enough. Henry's rasping shot rippled the net.

Gooooal! Henry Shefflin cracks in his 22nd championship goal! An absolute rocket!

Henry raised his arm, pointing his finger high into the sky.

'Yes, Sheff!' roared Eoin Larkin as he celebrated. 'I knew you'd do it!'

'The game's not won yet, lads. Keep going!' shouted Henry.

But Tipperary's hearts were broken. And seconds later came goal number two.

Gooooal! Comerford! Two in a row! The game has turned around!

Henry jumped into the air. That was it. There was no way back for Tipp now. The referee blew the final whistle. Kilkenny were the All-Ireland champions for the fourth time in a row. King Henry had done it again.

'Yeeesssss, Sheff!' roared Eddie Brennan as they hugged on the pitch.

'We did it!' said Henry, laughing. He was almost too exhausted to celebrate. He felt relief more than joy. Under all the pressure in the world, he had delivered. It was a sweet feeling.

As the fans flooded the Croke Park pitch, Henry found Brian Cody under the stand. It was now official. The greatest manager and greatest player in the game shared a quiet moment.

'Outstanding, Henry!' said Brian with a smile from ear to ear. 'I told you everything would be okay!'

'I'm glad you thought so,' laughed Henry. 'I wasn't so sure myself!'

***

Henry climbed the steps and raised the Liam McCarthy Cup high into the sky. All his dreams had come true and the celebrations were only beginning. But there was only one place Henry wanted to be now. Back home in Ballyhale, a small village halfway between Kilkenny and Waterford. The place where the story of King Henry began.

Chapter 2

Ballyhale Boy

The day Henry Shefflin was born, 11 January 1979, is a day that will live long in the history of Kilkenny hurling.

His mother, Mai, held the little baby boy in her arms and looked at him adoringly.

'Isn't he beautiful?' she said to her husband, Henry Senior. 'I could stare at him all day long.'

'Isn't he just,' said Henry Senior. 'A fine lad.'

Henry had light blue eyes that sparkled so brightly they were almost green. And traces of the red hair that would make him stand out on the pitch in years to come. It was also clear that he was a big strong boy.

'You might just grow up to be a fine hurler,' Henry Senior whispered into the baby's ear with a grin. 'A strapping centre-forward maybe.'

The little baby twitched and shook his hand in the air, as if he agreed.

'What will we call him?' asked Mai.

'Sure, Henry, of course!' said his dad straightaway. 'After me! There can't be enough Henry Shefflins in the world!'

They burst out laughing and little baby Henry smiled happily.

'Now let's bring him home,' said Mai.

Even though Henry's family were all from Kilkenny, he was actually born over the border in the neighbouring county, Waterford. Another great hurling county, and big rivals of Kilkenny. If the nurses and doctors knew then how good a hurler Henry would grow up to be, they might never have let him leave the hospital and cross the county border. But luckily for

Kilkenny, Henry was soon safely home in Ballyhale.

Already waiting for him were his two older brothers, John and Tommy, and his sisters, Cecilia, Aileen and Helena. His younger brother, Paul, would be born just over a year later. The family were at the centre of life in Ballyhale. And life in Ballyhale meant hurling.

Henry's dad was born and bred in Ballyhale and his family had lived there for generations. He was a talented hurler himself, but when he was a young man he moved to England in search of work. Even though not many people in England had heard of the great game of hurling, that didn't stop Henry Senior pursuing his passion. He joined a team of other Irish lads in a place called Warwickshire and they ended up getting all the way to an All-Ireland junior final way back in 1957.

But sadly, his dad died suddenly, so Henry Senior cut short his time in England to move home to Ballyhale to take over the family pub and farm. The pub was called Sheffs, and it would have a big impact on King Henry's life when he was growing up.

Henry Senior soon met Mai. She was from Glenmore in South Kilkenny, a village known for its battles with Ballyhale on the hurling field. Mai was from a family of five who all loved hurling. She played camogie and one of her brothers played for the Kilkenny minor team. So from the moment he was born, hurling was in Henry's blood whether he liked it or not. How could it be any other way?

Henry came into the world during a golden era of hurling, not just in Ballyhale but in Kilkenny too. The year before he was born, Ballyhale had won their first ever county title. In that campaign, seven Fennelly brothers, Ger, Kevin, Brendan, Mick, Seán, Liam and Dermot, scored all Ballyhale's goals and points on their way to glory.

Kilkenny were one of the best teams in the country at the time and they won the All-Ireland in 1979, beating Galway in the final. Kevin Fennelly was one of the stars of the team. So Henry didn't have to look too far for inspiration. Some of the best ever hurlers in the country were right on his doorstep in his home village. And before he had even turned one, Henry had seen Ballyhale lift a county title and Kilkenny take the All-Ireland crown, something many people wait for their whole life.

Chapter 3

Friary Field of Dreams

Henry learned how to hold a hurl and sliotar even before he could walk. He looked up to his older brothers, John and Tommy. They were ten and eight years older than him, so they were always coming and going to training and matches. Like all toddlers, Henry copied their every move. His sisters played camogie too. So there was no shortage of hurls, helmets and sliotars lying around the house. Henry didn't have to wander too far to find them. He'd sometimes pull on a Ballyhale jersey, five sizes too big for him, hanging down to his toes, and have a puck around in the house. He made everyone laugh. But even then, his family could see he had talent.

The family home was a busy place. The door was always open and there was usually somebody visiting. The pub and the house were one and the same. Friends, neighbours and strangers were as likely to call to the back door as the front. Henry soon got used to the coming and going and all the chat. He loved listening to the grown-ups talking. And because it was Ballyhale, the chat was usually about hurling.

As he got older, Henry was often sent to work in the bar, helping his mother, collecting and cleaning glasses. Sheffs was the place everyone went to after big matches in the village. Even the players would go there. Henry loved hearing them talk about the game they had just played. Who played well? More important, who didn't? Who got the winning score? Did they get the tactics right? It wasn't just work for young Henry, it was an education. He learned as much from those days working in the bar as he did on the training field. It made him want to be a hurler. He wanted to be the talk of the town and the talk of Sheffs when he grew up.

If Henry wasn't in the bar, he would usually be found on the farm with his dad. He loved the farming life. There was never a dull moment and there was always a job to be done. No matter what he was doing, Henry would always have a hurl in his hand. If they were checking on the cattle, fixing walls or walking the fields, Henry and his brother Paul would tag along, pucking and hopping balls. They couldn't pass a wall without hitting a few shots against it. It was simply their way of life.

On the rare occasions when they got a chance to escape the jobs at home, Henry and Paul would be allowed down to the local pitch to watch Ballyhale in action. The pitch was called Friary Field, and to young Henry it was every bit as amazing as Croke Park. That's where he watched the famous Fennelly brothers work their magic. They may have been known all over Ireland as stars of the game. But to Henry they were just locals. Later, as his older brothers grew up, he watched them togging out and playing for the village. Nothing filled him with more pride than seeing John or Tommy strike a perfect point.

'Wooooo! Well done, Tommy!', young Henry would shout from the sidelines. To him it was as good as an All-Ireland final. Henry couldn't wait for the day when he would be big enough to join his brothers. He dreamed of playing for Ballyhale and stepping out onto that glorious green grass.

After watching a match, Henry and his brother Paul would head straight out to the squash court behind their house. It was the perfect place for a puck around. There was a giant wall on three sides where they could smash the ball without any fear of breaking a window! Best of all, there were floodlights. So even when it was dark, Henry could go outside, striking frees and practising penalties.

Sometimes half the children in the village would be in there playing a match that seemed to go on for ever. Henry and his brother Paul would be right in the thick of the action. They'd pick teams and battle it out for the glory of winning. The odd time, they'd be on opposite sides. But mostly they preferred to play together. In Henry's mind they were just like their older brothers John and Tommy, playing for the senior team.

On one summer night there was a memorable game on the squash court. Henry was on one team and Paul on the other. It was a fierce contest with all the boys and girls mixed in together, trying to get a piece of the action. Henry was pulling off all his flicks and tricks. Scooping the sliotar and flicking it over for score after score. But his team were still behind. The floodlights were burning brightly and in Henry's mind he was playing an All-Ireland final for Kilkenny at Croke Park.

'HENRYYYY! PAAAAUL!' Time to come in for dinner!' his mam called from the house.

'Ah no, Mam!' roared Henry. 'Not now!'

'Looks like it's next goal the winner, then,' laughed Paul. 'If we don't go in, she'll turn off the lights anyway!'

'Right!' said Henry. 'Next goal the winner.'

He gathered his teammates into a huddle. This might be a fun game among friends but even here, winning meant everything to Henry.

'We're not losing this one. I can't have Paul slagging me all night long!'

The action started again and the hits were flying. Henry got his hands on the ball but he was hooked and blocked in a ferocious contest.

'Ah come on! That's a free!' roared Henry. But there was no referee here!

'Get up!' shouted Paul. It was getting tense.

Some ground hurling now and a few wild pulls. The pride of the village was on the line.

Suddenly Henry got on the ball again. He looked up and saw some space. He flicked the sliotar over his head and caught it.

Outrageous skill from Shefflin!

Now he was into space and racing clear. Paul was charging towards him, getting ready to make a big hit. But Henry skilfully stepped inside and avoided the challenge. Now he was in on goal. Only the keeper to beat. He took aim and fired.

Goooooal! Shefflin does it again!

Henry jumped and punched the air. His teammates ran to surround him.

'Yesssss! We did it!' he shouted.

'Fair play, Henry. But I'll get you next time,' groaned Paul. He hated losing to Henry.

Just then the floodlights went out. The goal had come in the nick of time. They'd better go home for tea or there'd be big trouble.

After a big feed it was time for bed. Henry and Paul shared a bed in the attic in the same room as John and Tommy. Sometimes it was so cold they had to huddle together to keep warm. As they pulled on their pyjamas, the talk was still of hurling and the game on the squash court. As Henry's head hit the pillow he began to dream of his winning goal, except this time he was a grown-up, wearing the famous black and amber of Kilkenny. And he was scoring the goal on All-Ireland final day at Croke Park.

Chapter 4

St Patrick's

The first day of school is a nervous time for most children. But Henry had nothing to worry about when he started at St Patrick's. For a start, he didn't have far to travel. Just out of the back door of his house, past the squash court and across two fields. He had no excuse to be late for class! And he already knew a lot of the children from the village.

Henry loved school from the start. Not just because it was a great place to learn reading, writing and maths. But, much more important, St Patrick's was a great place to study the game of hurling.

Henry came under the spell of the school principal, Mr Dunphy. He knew everything there was to know about hurling and he was a great teacher. Henry was about to become his star pupil. He started to play proper, organised games, learning tactics and positioning to add to the skills he already knew from pucking around at home. Henry was hooked on hurling.

His first match for the school came one Wednesday evening. This was the moment he had dreamed of. The night before the game, he got everything ready. He polished his boots until they were so shiny he could almost see his face in them. He tightened the straps on his helmet. He tightly wrapped the grip on his hurl. Then he asked his big brother John for some advice.

'What's it like playing a real game?' he said.

'Just treat it the same as a puck around out the back, Henry. Just play your own game,' replied John.

But Henry was too excited. All day long he couldn't wait for school to end. He paid no attention in class that day. His head was filled with dreams of the big match. When the time came he ran to the pitch as fast as his legs could carry him. His jersey was so long it almost tripped him up. Henry didn't make the starting team but that didn't dent his enthusiasm. As the match was on, he followed Mr Dunphy up and down the touchline, his jersey hanging down below his knees.

'Sir, Sir, Sir! Can you put me on?' he pleaded.

Eventually the time came and he crossed the white line. He was in at corner-forward, just where he wanted to be. And within seconds he made his mark.

Henry was younger than most of the players and smaller too. But he used quick thinking to outsmart the opposition. A breaking ball flashed in front of the square and Henry didn't need a second invitation.

Goooooal! Shefflin whips it into the net from close range!

Henry was off the mark. It felt so good. Now he wanted more.

He learned a lot from the massive games that all the school kids played on their lunch break. Huge rolling games with all the pupils mucking in together, whatever their age or size. Henry learned how to handle some heavy hits there. It toughened him up for bigger battles ahead.

One day Henry was in action on the school pitch. He was showing off his latest tricks and flicks. His brother Paul was on the other team and he took no prisoners. He hit Henry a wallop.

Owwwwwww!

'Fair shoulder!' shouted Paul. And play carried on.

Henry dusted himself down. But he didn't want to continue. He was sore and he didn't like it. Then out of the corner of his eye he saw his dad watching. The school was so close to his house that Henry Senior would often walk over and watch the games. He loved keeping an eye on Henry and Paul.

When Henry got home that night, his dad had a few words for him.

'I saw what happened today, Henry,' he said quietly. 'It's never nice getting hit but it's part of the game. You have to be tough and strong. Don't let them know they're getting to you. Stand up and play on. But play fair. The best way to hurt them is by scoring a goal. That's how you get revenge.'

Henry knew he was right. His dad was always so encouraging.

'Thanks, Dad. I'll know next time,' Henry said, as he went off to bed to rest his tired body.

Henry didn't have to learn his lessons twice. He listened to everything Mr Dunphy had to say. All the children in the school did. And soon they became a proper team. They started to play in the Kilkenny championship against other schools and Henry was now tasting competitive action. This meant travelling around the county. Which sometimes brought problems of its own.

One day they had a match in a place called Muckalee, a long way from Ballyhale. Henry's mam drove Henry and some of his friends to the match. But she got lost on the way.

'Come on, Mam! Where are you going?' said Henry, fuming.

'You can get out and walk if you'd like,' said his mam crossly.

The other boys thought it was gas. They were trying to hold in the laughter. Henry was raging. He was so worried he would miss the start of the game. In the end, they just about made it. But Henry learned an important lesson. Never leave anything to chance. Always be prepared for the worst.

That was the start of a special journey for Henry and the St Patrick's school team.

Chapter 5

Lisdowney Sevens

Under the watchful eye of Mr Dunphy, Henry and the school team slowly began to learn the recipe for hurling success. They had other talented players too, like Aidan Cummins and Bob Aylward, who played alongside Henry. But they all had a lot to learn.

The first year together they played in the third tier of Kilkenny Schools, Roinn C. They lost more games than they won. Mr Dunphy taught them that talent wasn't everything.

They had to work for each other and learn the tactics of the game too. The following year, they improved a little and were promoted for the next season to Roinn B. The matches were harder now. They were playing against better players.

They all had to step up and improve their game, but sometimes Henry grew impatient and tried to do too much on his own. He had to learn to trust his teammates.

'It's not all about you, Henry!' Mr Dunphy told him sternly one day.

The hours on the training pitch were starting to pay off. St Patrick's were starting to click a little. They were growing, improving and working hard all the time. The first year in Roinn B was tough. But the next year they were much better. Soon Henry and the boys had winners' medals in their back pocket. It was a great feeling. It was Henry's first medal, and it gave him a taste for more.

The next year, Henry and his teammates moved up to Roinn A. Things were getting serious now. This would be a much bigger challenge. They were playing against the best school teams and players in the county. It was a struggle at first. Henry hated losing, but that's what was happening every week. The boys on the other teams seemed bigger and stronger. Henry wondered if maybe he had picked the wrong game. He wondered if he was really good enough to make it as a hurler.

But he stuck at it. He trained hard, listened to what Mr Dunphy said and he grew a bit taller too. By the time he was in sixth class, he was getting better week by week and starting to make a name for himself on the hurling field. Teachers from the other schools were starting to notice his talent.

'Watch out for the big lad up front,' they would tell their team before games.

'Don't let the corner-forward out of your sight. He's dangerous!'

'The big lad with the red hair has some skill!'

Henry took the attention in his stride. He had all the talent but he was never big-headed.

He was willing to listen, learn and work hard. That was the secret of success.

The talk about Henry went into overdrive when he played a starring role at the Lisdowney Sevens. It's a big tournament played every year. All the clubs in Kilkenny come to battle to be the best. Henry knew it was his chance to shine.

St Patrick's had a great team and waltzed through the competition. They won their matches easily and Henry was scoring for fun. But there were no celebrations. They were here to win. They made it all the way to the final. They would be coming up against Ballingarry.

'Now, lads, this is another step up,' said Mr Dunphy as he stood in a huddle of players in the middle of the pitch. 'These are a serious outfit. We'll have to be at our best to beat them.'

'Come on, lads. We've worked too hard to let it slip now,' said Henry quietly to his teammates as he slapped his hurl into the palm of his hand. They knew he meant business. But they didn't know just how good he was going to be.

The referee blew the whistle and the game was on. There was a big crowd watching on from the sideline and nobody would ever forget what they saw that day.

St Patrick's tore into the game, sprinting, stretching and shouldering with all their might. Ballingarry knew they were in a game. Mr Dunphy always said you had to earn the right to play hurling. Win the battle first and then you can show your skills. St Patrick's were doing that today. Nobody more than Henry. It was one of those games where everything seemed to go right for him.

He leapt like a salmon to catch the sliotar in the middle and slotted it over the bar. He made it look so simple. Point after point, everything he hit went straight over the bar. But Ballingarry weren't giving up. The teams were level in the closing stages, when St Patrick's got a sideline ball. Henry stood over it and there was only one thought on his mind. He knew straightaway what he was going to do.

He stood still and took a deep breath. His heart was thumping in his chest. He was way out on the right touchline. Surely it was too far out to go over, even for an inter-county player, never mind a schoolboy. But Henry had no doubts. Time seemed to slow down. All eyes were on him but he didn't feel the pressure. He believed 100 per cent in what was going to happen.

He stepped back from the sliotar and took a step to the side. He plucked a few blades of grass from the pitch and threw them into the air to check which way the wind was blowing. He looked up to the posts and back down at the ball. He stuck his hurl into the ground and bent it just a little. Then he took two more steps back and stopped to look up at the posts again. His breathing was calm now.

'Okay, go!' he said to himself.

He took two quick steps forward and swung his hurl. He made a perfect connection, slicing right under the sliotar and sending it high. It flew through the air, spinning in an arc. Just like he had pictured it. He watched it all the way. The crowd gasped. The Ballingarry players could only watch on in despair. The sliotar flew straight between the posts.

He's done it! What a sideline cut from the young maestro Shefflin!

Henry raised his arm in delight and punched the air. The referee blew his whistle. St Patrick's had won the cup!

His teammates ran over to celebrate. Cummins was first to jump on his back.

'Unreal, Henry!' he roared.

Next was Aylward, slapping him on the back.

'You fluked it!' he laughed. 'No way you were trying to score from there!'

Henry had produced one of the most magical displays of hurling ever seen from a young boy. The grown-ups watching couldn't believe their eyes. 'This lad is something else!'

Henry was delighted. For himself, for his teammates, but most of all for Mr Dunphy. He had taught them all about the game and made them into a great team. Henry didn't know a better way to repay him than to win the cup. Everyone in the school went wild celebrating. And best of all, they got no homework for a week. Henry was the hero!

Chapter 6

Small Fish in a Big Pond

After so much success at school with St Patrick's it was time for Henry to focus on the club. Ballyhale had the best team in Ireland when Henry was growing up. Now he too was following in the footsteps of the great Fennelly brothers. He was so excited. He couldn't have been in a better place to grow as a hurler.

His friends from school were with him on this new journey too. Cummins, Aylward and Tom Coogan too. But the club game was much more difficult than school matches. The hits were harder and space was tighter. It was a real eye opener. Henry and the boys had to toughen up. And quickly.

It took some time. Henry wondered again if he had what it took to be a top hurler. But slowly, he started to get used to the rough and tumble. He was almost starting to enjoy the hits. They all were. It was another big step in his life as a hurler.

Ballyhale eventually made their way to the county final, where they came up against their neighbours and big rivals Thomastown. It was another tough, tense battle as it always was when you played a local team. Henry was getting some rough attention and it wasn't going his way.

'Hang in there, Henry. Keep going!' roared Aylward when he saw Henry's head starting to drop.

Henry knew he had to keep going, no matter what. Soon the game began to change. Ballyhale were on top now and Henry found his rhythm again. His frees started to float between the posts. Before long, the sides were level. There was nothing between them with minutes to go. Ballyhale were pushing hard for a winner. But Thomastown were throwing the kitchen sink at them in return. With seconds left Thomastown were leading by two points. Ballyhale needed a goal, and quickly. Then suddenly came the sharp *peep peep* of the referee's whistle.

It's a penalty to Ballyhale! Out of the blue!

Henry stepped up straightaway. There was no doubt in his mind he was going to score. It had to hit the back of the net. He eyeballed the Thomastown goalkeeper. There were two more defenders on the line. Henry picked his spot and decided to go for power. 'Pick your spot and don't change your mind,' his dad once told him. So that's what he did.

He went through his usual routine. Slowed his breathing. Took two steps forward, lifted the sliotar, took aim and fired.

What a save! Shefflin has missed the penalty. Heartbreak for Ballyhale!

Henry couldn't believe it. It was the last puck of the game and he had missed. 'Chin up, Sheff,' said Cummins as he put his arm around him. 'Happens to the best.'

Henry wanted to be anywhere but out on that pitch. He felt sick as the Thomastown players celebrated. He buried his head in his hands. He wanted to cry. Winning was the best feeling on earth. But losing was the worst.

***

Henry's disappointment lasted for days. He was no fun to be around at home. He kept thinking about his penalty miss over and over again. He did the only thing he knew to deal with it. He spent hours on end out the back in the squash court. Hitting the penalty again and again until he got it right. Practising until he felt his arms would fall off with tiredness. He was upset. But so long as he had a ball, a wall and a hurl, he would be okay.

A few days later his sadness turned to joy. He got something unexpected in the post when he came home from school.

'There's a letter for you, Henry,' his mam told him when he came in the door.

'A letter? For me?' he asked. 'Who's it from?'

'His secret admirer!' joked his sister. 'Is it a Valentine's card?'

'Get lost,' snapped Henry, snatching the letter.

'Well, I suppose you'll have to open it, won't you?' said his mam with a glint in her eye.

Henry opened the envelope slowly, being careful not to tear the paper inside. He unfolded the page and started to read it. The top right-hand corner had the Kilkenny GAA crest on it. His hand started to shake a little.

Dear Henry, it began.

He read on, hardly believing the words in front of him. The letter was from the Kilkenny County Board. They wanted him to play for the Kilkenny under-14s. Was this real? He had to read the letter twice to be sure. He was going to follow in the footsteps of his big brothers John and Tommy and wear the famous black and amber striped jersey of Kilkenny.

'Well? Are you going to tell me who it's from?' his mam finally asked.

'Kilkenny ... I'm ... I'm going to play for the county team, Mam. I can't believe it!' said Henry with tears in his eyes.

'I'm so proud of you. You deserve it. I can't believe you're all grown up now, Henry,' his mam said as she pulled him in for a big hug.

Henry sat down to tea with a huge smile on his face. This was it. The moment he had always dreamed of.

A few weeks later he travelled with the Kilkenny under-14 squad to the Tony Forristal Tournament in Waterford. All the best young players in the country were there. It was time for Henry to see if he really was good enough for the top.

His big chance came against Wexford and Henry was more than ready to show everyone what he was made of. The going was tough early on. The Wexford boys seemed bigger, faster and stronger than anyone he had played against before. But he was playing with the best of Kilkenny now too. He knew he would get plenty of ball and plenty of chances to score. He just had to take them.

Suddenly a low ball was slipped inside to the forward line. Henry was tightly marked but gathered it quickly and spun towards goal. He got a fierce slap of the hurl across his hand but he slipped his marker and was barrelling in on goal. The defender was breathing down his neck looking for a hook. So Henry, quick as a flash, shortened the grip on his hurl and let fly from close range.

Goooooal! Great skill from Shefflin!

Soon he was in again. This time he showed off his talents in the air. Gathering a high ball and using his strength to shuffle away from the defender. He was further out, so had to go for power. He fired it with all the force he had.

Goooooal! Number two for Shefflin and Kilkenny! A star is born!

The tournament ended in disappointment for Kilkenny. Even though they had skilful players, they didn't click as a team and failed to make the semi-finals. But Henry had made his mark with two goals and a point. He thought things would be easy for him now. Little did he know how wrong he was.

Chapter 7

St Kieran's College

It was almost time for Henry to leave St Patrick's. He had to start thinking about secondary school. For any young lad in Kilkenny who was obsessed with hurling, there was only one place to go. St Kieran's College, the home of hurling.

Henry's older brothers had gone there too. When he was younger, he used to go to watch them play for the school. The great DJ Carey was the star of the St Kieran's team. He was unbelievably talented and would grow up to be a huge star. Even back then he was the standout player. There was no doubt in Henry's mind that he would go to St Kieran's when the time came.

There was only one obstacle in the way. He had to do the entrance exam. He came out in a cold sweat at the thought. He knew it was going to be tough, but it would be worth it if he could follow in the footsteps of all the great Kilkenny hurlers. He studied hard in the weeks and days before the exam. He practised his English, Irish and maths. But it was hard going. He wasn't great for hitting the books at the best of times. He wished the tests were about pucking and catching a sliotar, rather than spellings and sums.

He had a knot in his stomach on the day of the exam as he sat down in the big hall with all the other boys. This was worse than taking a vital penalty for his team, he thought.

'Good luck, Henry!' said Mr Dunphy, giving him a thumbs-up as he walked past his desk.

'I'm going to need it,' said Henry nervously.

Then he turned over the page and got to work. It was exhausting. He really struggled with some of the questions. He tried his best to answer but there were times when his mind went blank. It wasn't good at all. When the time was up he sat back in his chair and puffed out his cheeks.

Pheeewww!

'I'm glad that's over,' he smiled to the boy next to him. He knew in his heart he hadn't done his best. He had been too nervous.

A few days later the results came in. He anxiously opened the envelope with the slip of paper inside. Henry's worst fears had come true. His gut instinct was right. He had done badly in the exams.

'Oh no!' he thought. 'I'll never get into Kieran's with these results.'

'My mam and dad are going to be so cross,' he said to Cummins and Aylward.

'Don't worry, Henry, it'll all work out.'

Henry went to see Mr Dunphy in his office.

'What am I going to do?' he asked with his head in his hands. He was heartbroken.

'Listen Henry, I have an idea,' said Mr Dunphy.

'I don't think you did yourself justice in the exams,' he said. 'You're better than these results.'

'Yeah, I think you're right,' said Henry. 'I just got all jumpy and I couldn't think straight.'

'So here's the plan,' Mr Dunphy replied with a smile. 'You're still young enough to play primary schools hurling again next year. Why don't you repeat sixth class? That way you can play for the school team for another year and you can repeat the entrance exam for St Kieran's again next year. With another year of lessons behind you, you'll fly through it.'

'Wow! That's the best idea I've ever heard,' laughed Henry. 'Do you think my mam and dad will go for it?'

'Don't worry about them, Henry!' smiled Mr Dunphy.

That night Henry told his mam and dad the

bad news about the entrance exam and then ran Mr Dunphy's idea by them.

'I don't see any reason why not,' said his mam. 'Another year here in Ballyhale will do you no harm.'

'It'll be great for your schooling. And, more important, your hurling!' his dad said with a wink.

Henry felt instantly relieved. Everyone was happy. He got to hurl for St Patrick's for another year. The school got another year out of their best player. And now he was in the same class as his younger brother Paul. It was win, win, win as far as Henry was concerned.

And when the time came, Henry was a year older and wiser, and he passed the entrance exam with flying colours. He was finally off to St Kieran's to follow in the footsteps of his brothers and the great DJ Carey.

***

Henry had worked hard to get to St Kieran's, so he made sure he enjoyed his new surroundings. He was good in school, without being great. He enjoyed learning new subjects. He loved his new teachers Mr Walsh and Mr Hogan. Just like Henry, they preferred to be outside hurling than stuck inside in class.

Most of the boys arrived to school 45 minutes early for the first game of the day before lessons began. They would squeeze in another 10 minutes at break and another half an hour at lunchtime. There was always time for another quick puck about. Even when they waited for the bus home they would have a game. Every pupil in St Kieran's had a hurl in their hand almost all the time. Henry was right at home.

But even though he loved going to school at St Kieran's, he started to struggle on the pitch. He didn't know why. He just started to lose his touch a little. He wasn't making his mark in games like he usually did. He had done well in Ballyhale. But now he was playing against the best from all over the county. He was a small fish in a big pond. He lost his confidence and no longer felt like the main man on the pitch. He started to get substituted during games. Something that had never happened to him before. And then he was dropped from the team. That was a huge shock. He had always been an automatic pick, one of the first names on the team sheet. But not now. It was a new experience for Henry, and he didn't like it.

He complained to his friends, his teachers, his brothers and sisters and his mam and dad. But they all gave him the same message. He knew it himself. He had to do what he always did. Keep his head down and work hard. Train more, hit the gym, eat the right food. Listen to his coaches and ask what he could do to improve. Even though Henry had all the skill in the world, it was his work rate that marked him out above all the other players. When the going gets tough, the tough get going. So that's what Henry did.

By the time he reached fifth year, Henry was back in business. He had grown a lot and was now able to handle the rough and tumble.

He was stronger too, and he had matured. Early that year he had a memorable game on the training pitch where everything he touched turned to gold. His confidence was back. The hard work had paid off and he was once more a star forward in the team.

St Kieran's were up against St Peter's College from Wexford in the Leinster semi-final. They were expected to win well and Henry was hoping it might be a good day to rack up some scores. But it all went wrong early on. St Kieran's were on the attack and a high cross-field ball was aimed right in at Henry. He pulled off a trademark jump high into the sky and caught the ball perfectly. But a St Peter's defender had jumped with him. He was a big lad and he landed right on Henry's toe.

Owwwwwww!

The physio ran straight to Henry but there was nothing he could do.

'It's a broken toe, Henry. At least eight weeks out.'

Henry felt crushed as he hopped off the

pitch. He didn't even feel the pain any more, only the disappointment of the games he was going to miss.

He worked hard at his physio exercises and tried to keep his fitness up. That was hard because he couldn't run. He had to watch on from the sidelines as St Kieran's won the Leinster title against Good Counsel from Wexford. He was delighted for his teammates but he didn't join in the celebrations. He didn't feel part of it when he hadn't played in the game. His only focus now was on recovering in time for the schools All-Ireland final.

St Kieran's swept aside St Mary's from Belfast in the All-Ireland semi-final. Henry felt sick to have to sit it out. He was nearly fit and ready to play again, but it was a race against time. He did everything he could to help his toe heal faster. Resting, putting ice on it, physio. With just a week to go to the game he declared himself fit.

'Are you sure, Henry?' asked the team's manager, Mr Philpott.

'If I say I'm ready, I'm ready,' said Henry.

Mr Philpott wasn't sure. But he could see in Henry's face how much he wanted to play.

Henry did well in training. That proved he was fit, if not quite back to his best. A couple of days before the big game the team sheet was pinned to the noticeboard on the wall in school. Like the rest of the boys, Henry raced over to see it. He scanned the page going from the goalkeeper, to the backs numbers 2 to 7, the midfielders 8 and 9, then the forwards. He wasn't picked at 11, 12 or 13 with the half-forwards. His eyes read on quickly. Number 13? Not there, Number 14, full-forward? No. Number 15? H. Shefflin.

'Yes!' Henry let out a big sigh of relief. He had just made it. The last name on the team sheet. But there he was. He was starting an All-Ireland final.

The journey to Croke Park was like nothing Henry had ever experienced before. He had been there before, but only to watch. The first time he went to Croke Park was when he was a very small boy. Kilkenny were playing Galway in the All-Ireland final. He sat on his dad's lap throughout the game. He couldn't believe the size of the crowd, all the fans dressed in different colours, cheering on their teams. He thought Croke Park was the most magical place on earth. It was the most exciting day of his life, even though Kilkenny lost. Now, 10 years later, he was going to Croke Park again. This time he was going to play.

The craic was mighty on the bus up to Dublin. St Kieran's had a brilliant team. As well as Henry and his brother Paul, they had Seán Dowling, Michael Kavanagh, Henry's old primary school friend Aidan Cummins, Willie Maher and captain Davey Carroll. The best in Kilkenny at that age. Henry considered them his friends as well as his teammates. There were some Tipperary and Laois players as well. They had quality all over the field.

But their opponents were talented too. St Colman's from Fermoy in Cork was a well-known hurling school. They had a star centre-forward, Timmy McCarthy, who would go on to be a huge player for Cork when he got older.

Mr Philpott was worried before the game. He thought there was too much messing on the bus.

'Okay, lads. It's time to focus,' he said as the bus arrived at the gates of Croke Park. Here they were. The home of Gaelic games. Henry just hoped his toe would be okay.

All the pupils from St Kieran's had made the trip to cheer on Henry and his teammates. They were dancing and singing songs in the stands. It was a great day out. There was a huge roar as the teams ran out onto the pitch.

Henry felt the lush grass under his boots. He looked around to take it all in. Croke Park. Just like he imagined it. His dream come true.

The game began and it seemed Mr Philpott was right. St Kieran's weren't at the races. Colman's were much the better team and Henry could only look on as they ripped through their defence. Corner-forward Will

O'Donoghue scored two quick-fire goals. At half-time it looked all over. Colman's were ahead by 2-5 to 7 points.

Kieran's didn't give up in the second-half but they were running out of time. After 46 minutes Padraig Delaney earned a 65. Davey Carroll went out to take it. Henry had a quick word.

'Just lob it in, Davey. Edge of the square,' he whispered.

That's exactly what Davey did. There was an almighty scramble and up popped Willie Maher with the sliotar. He flicked it over his head as quick as a flash.

Goooooal!

'Yes, Willie!' roared Henry. They were back in the match.

Henry stuck over a point of his own in the closing stages and St Kieran's held on for the win.

The whistle blew and the crowd went wild. Henry dropped to his knees. He couldn't take it in at first. But he didn't feel any pain in his toe now.

'Yeeeessss!' roared Cummins as he charged towards Henry. 'All-Ireland champions, baby!'

The team travelled back to Kilkenny singing and dancing on the bus. The whole school went out on the Sunday night to celebrate. It was Henry's first taste of major success and he liked it.

Chapter 8

Big Trouble

Hurling was Henry's life, but it wasn't the only sport he played. He was a keen Gaelic footballer and even played for the Kilkenny minors, scoring a famous goal to spark a great comeback against Laois in the first round of the Leinster minor football championship. Henry was a good footballer. Perhaps if he had been from another county, like Kerry or Dublin, then maybe he could have become a star of the big ball game. But in Kilkenny, and Ballyhale in particular, the sliotar was the only ball that mattered.

He loved soccer too. He played for his local team, Southend United, and the school team. He was a big forward and had a knack of finding the back of the net. He always dreamed of playing for Arsenal. But he knew he wasn't quick enough to make it as a professional soccer player. His brother Tommy was a Liverpool fan, so there was always great slagging between them at home. He would never forget the night Arsenal won the English Football League ahead of Liverpool. There had been nothing between the two teams all season. It came down to the final match at Anfield, Liverpool's home stadium. Arsenal had to win by at least two goals to win the league.

Nobody gave Arsenal a chance. The Liverpool team was full of stars, including the brilliant Irish players Steve Staunton, Ronnie Whelan, Ray Houghton and John Aldridge. But Henry was hoping for a miracle as he sat down to watch the match with his brothers. Arsenal had David O'Leary, the elegant Irish defender, and star striker Alan Smith, who Henry loved watching. Arsenal took the lead just before half-time. Smith with a header. Henry was getting excited.

'We're coming for you, Tommy!' he laughed. His brother was starting to get nervous.

But Arsenal couldn't get a second goal no matter how hard they tried. As the game went into the closing seconds, it looked like Liverpool would win the league. But then midfielder Michael Thomas took a chance and ran towards the box. The ball broke to him and he charged on towards goal. He picked his spot.

Goooooal!

The most dramatic goal in the history of English soccer. Henry jumped off the couch and almost punched the lampshade. Amazing! Arsenal were champions with the final kick of the game! His brother Tommy was sick. He sat staring at the screen in disbelief.

Henry wouldn't let it go. He ran around the house for a week singing 'We Are the

Champions' just to wind Tommy up. It was great craic. But it also taught Henry an important lesson about sport. You always have to keep going to the final whistle and never give up. It was a lesson he would remember throughout his career with Kilkenny.

Away from the pitch, Henry loved having the craic. He took his sport seriously, but if there was devilment to be had, Henry would be in the middle of it. A bit of messing around at school or tearing around the village on his bike. Sometimes he'd be missing for hours on end up the land, getting up to mischief with his brothers or his friends. One time, he took things a bit too far.

It was the weekend of the Leinster hurling final between Kilkenny and Offaly. As it happened, Henry was playing an under-16 hurling blitz in Dublin. The best young players from all over Leinster were there and Henry was the star of the show. He had an unbelievable tournament. He scored four goals and a point against Dublin.

Then in the next match against Galway he grabbed an early goal and a point. He was flying. Just before half-time he jumped high for a ball. A Galway back had a wild pull at the ball and missed. The last thing Henry saw was a hurl swinging straight towards his face.

Smasshhhhhh!

His eye split open and there was blood everywhere. Henry was rushed straight to hospital in an ambulance. He was terrified. He sat in the hospital bed as the doctor examined him.

'How did it happen?'

'I really don't know,' said Henry. 'I can hardly remember.'

He had been wearing a helmet, but no faceguard. Now he regretted that.

'Will I be okay?' he asked the doctor. He couldn't see at all now and was getting worried.

'It's too soon to say,' the doctor replied.

Henry sat there all alone wondering if he was ever going to be able to see again. Never mind play hurling. He was so frightened.

He was given some eye drops and they finally discovered he had burst a blood vessel. It was painful, but he was going to be okay. He was told to stay in bed and get some rest. He felt very lonesome in a big hospital in Dublin on his own. But he was glad his hurling career wasn't over before it started.

The following morning, a pile of visitors arrived from Kilkenny. His brothers John and Tommy and their friends all called to see him. They had come to Dublin for the Leinster final at Croke Park. Kilkenny were playing Offaly.

'How are you feeling?' asked Tommy.

'Not a bother now,' replied Henry. 'A bit sore, but I'll live. At least I can see.'

They all laughed.

'Do you fancy coming with us? To Croke Park? Might cheer you up,' said John.

Henry didn't have to be asked twice. He jumped out of the bed and ran over to the nurse on duty.

'Any chance I can get out of here? I'm feeling much better,' he said.

'Not a hope!' replied the nurse. 'You nearly lost your eye. You'll have to stay in bed and rest for a few days.'

But Henry was having none of it. As soon as the nurse turned her back, he packed up his bag and slipped out of the hospital with the lads. They roared laughing all the way to Croke Park. Nothing was going to stop Henry watching Kilkenny in action. Even if he could hardly see.

He was in big trouble when he got home. His eye had swollen up again. Worse still, the nurse had called his mam from Dublin, telling her what Henry had done.

'How could you be so stupid?' she asked him.

Henry was back in hospital for the next few days. He learned his lesson the hard way.

Chapter 9

Time to Shine

After winning the schools All-Ireland final with St Kieran's, Henry started to get a lot more attention. He grew again over the summer and filled out a bit more. He was becoming a man and it started to show on the pitch too.

He was playing senior hurling now for Ballyhale and he had a lot to learn. He was still only a teenager and he was playing against much older men. But he could hold his own. He enjoyed the rough and tumble and taking the hits. His old schoolmates Aylward and Cummins were alongside him as always, and so was his brother Paul. They went on a winning streak and Henry was their chief marksman, scoring goal after goal and point after point. It wasn't long before he came to the attention of the Kilkenny minors.

His career in the black and amber jersey of Kilkenny didn't exactly start as he expected. He was sub goalie. Not what he dreamed of when he was a little boy. He wanted to score goals, not stop them. He wanted to follow in the footsteps of his hero, DJ Carey. But there was no point complaining. At least he was there, rubbing shoulders with the best players of his age in the county. He knew he just had to do what he had always done. Keep his head down and work hard. He was certain his talent would eventually shine through.

He kept playing well for the club back in Ballyhale. His scoring streak was so good that Kilkenny could no longer ignore him. In one match he scored three goals and seven points against a team from Gowran. Each score better than the last.

Goal ... Goal ... Goal ... Shefflin is unstoppable!

As luck would have it, there was a reporter from the local newspaper the *Kilkenny People* there. She wrote about Henry's brilliant performance. It was the talk of Kilkenny, and Henry was about to get his big chance. At training that week the boss called him over.

'You're starting on Sunday, Henry. Up top. You'd better be ready,' he said.

Henry was lost for words. He was about to play Dublin in the Leinster minor final. From sub goalie to starting forward in one giant leap. Just like that. He could hardly believe it.

The big day out didn't exactly go to plan. Henry was starved of ball all day and only managed to score one point before he was taken off. Kilkenny won, but Henry didn't feel like celebrating. In the next round, Kilkenny lost to Galway and were knocked out of the competition. Henry thought maybe he'd blown his big chance. He was really upset. Just when it looked like he was getting somewhere, he was back to square one. Not for the first time, he wondered if his dream would ever come true.

Chapter 10

Senior Hurling

At the end of the season, Henry was due to move to Waterford IT to start college and he thought about spending the summer in America. But out of nowhere, he was called up to the Kilkenny intermediates. It was a lifeline. He had another chance. This time he wasn't going to let it slip. He decided to stay at home, and got a summer job working in an electrical factory, so that he could continue to train and play hurling.

He scored a few frees in his first game for the intermediates and soon found himself in a Leinster final against Wexford. It was a special moment for the family when Henry lined out with his brother Tommy. It was a game they remember for all the wrong reasons, though. Tommy had a heavy fall and hit his face on the ground with full force.

Owwwwwww!

He smashed his mouth and six of his teeth fell out. Henry was first over to help him. He picked up the teeth from the grass and held them in his hand. It was a sharp reminder that hurling at this level was tougher than anything he'd faced before.

Things soon got better, though. Henry's summer of a lifetime took another twist when he was called up to play for the Kilkenny under-21s. They beat Dublin in a Leinster final before losing heavily to Galway in the All-Ireland semi-final. Henry was heartbroken again. But he had played manfully in defeat and scored an impressive three goals and four points. In just a few short weeks he'd gone from the minors, to intermediate, to the under-21s. There was only one more step to go now. It was surely only a matter of time before he was called up to the Kilkenny senior team.

At the end of the summer, he packed his bags and headed for his new life in college in Waterford.

Henry moved into a house with four other lads and they became great friends. There was always some kind of prank going on. Henry loved the craic. One morning he woke up to find all the furniture in the house was gone. One of the lads had moved it all in the middle of the night to a house down the road! They roared laughing about it all day. Although he was there to study, most of Henry's early days at college were spent hurling or having fun. But the time for messing was about to end.

One day he got a phone call out of the blue.

'Henry. Johnny Walsh here.'

'Hiya, Johnny,' said Henry. He knew Johnny well from Ballyhale. More important, he was one of the Kilkenny selectors.

'We'd like you to come up to Kilkenny training. Cody wants to have a look at you,' said Johnny.

Henry was speechless.

'Thanks, Johnny. I'd love to, thanks,' he finally got the words out. 'I'll need a lift up, though.'

'Don't worry, Henry,' laughed Johnny. 'I'll bring you.'

Brian Cody had just taken over as manager of Kilkenny and he was giving a few new faces the chance to shine. Henry was one of the lucky ones. A few days later he was togging out at Kilkenny training and stepping onto the same field as the great DJ Carey.

'Howya, Henry! Welcome to the club!' said DJ, smiling at Henry.

'Thanks, DJ!' said Henry, grinning from ear to ear. He had to pinch himself. Was he really about to play alongside the great DJ Carey? Was this really happening? Or was it a dream?

'Right, Henry! Snap out of it!' barked Cody

from the sideline. 'Time to show us what you can do!'

This was it. He was a Kilkenny player now. But he knew he had his work cut out to impress Brian Cody.

Chapter 11

Cody's Kilkenny

In the new year, Cody called out to Henry.

'Stay behind after training, Henry. I want a word!' he roared.

'This isn't good,' thought Henry. 'I hope I'm not in trouble.'

The other lads were winding him up.

'That's never a good thing, Sheff!' laughed McGarry, the team's goalkeeper.

At the end of the session, Henry made his way over to Cody.

'You've been going well in training Henry. I think it's time to see what you can do in the heat of battle. You're starting on Sunday!'

Henry could hardly speak, he was so excited. His first senior start in a Kilkenny jersey!

'Thanks, Brian,' he managed to stammer.

'Don't thank me now,' said Cody. 'Thank me with your performance on the pitch.'

Kilkenny were playing Wexford in an early season Walsh Cup clash in Mullinavat. It was a wet and windy night. A long way from the glamour of Croke Park in the summer. But to Henry it was the only place to be. DJ Carey wasn't playing, so Henry was given the responsibility of taking frees. He was nervous. But once the first one sailed over, he began to settle. He held his own and did enough to keep his starting place for the league.

When DJ returned to the team, Henry was kept on free-taking duty. A huge vote of confidence in him. Kilkenny's first match in the league was against Cork. One of the best teams in the country, with fine players like Timmy McCarthy and Mark Landers. It was a tough start for Henry, but he was determined to take every chance to shine. An early point settled him. And then came his big opportunity. Ten minutes from the end Ken O'Shea fizzed a pass right into Henry. He scooped it up and turned to face goal, 10 metres out. There was no time to think. Instinct took over. He had only one thing on his mind.

Goooooal! The new boy scores on his debut!

'Yesssss!' Henry jumped and punched the air. His first goal for the Cats. What a feeling!

He finished with a goal and four points, even though Kilkenny were on the losing side. He was starting to feel like he belonged at this level.

He scored six points in the next outing against Waterford, then six more as Kilkenny thumped Tipperary. Henry was making his mark. But the next match against Wexford was when everybody really started to sit up and take notice. It was Easter Sunday at Nowlan Park, the home of Kilkenny hurling.

Henry had a day to remember, but the Wexford corner-back had one to forget. Henry turned him inside and out so often that his blood was twisted by the end of the game.

A goooooal! And three more points for Shefflin. A superstar in the making!

Henry was having so much fun. Everything felt natural. Towards the end of the game, he scooped up the sliotar and flicked it over the heads of the Wexford backs before collecting it again. The crowd let out a huge gasp and a roar of excitement.

Olé, olé, olé!

Henry loved every second of it. He felt he was born to be here.

But disappointment soon followed the Wexford game. In the semi-final against Galway, Henry scored eight points, but Kilkenny lost. The team fell short.

Even though Kilkenny didn't go all the way that season, Henry was pleased with his own performances in the league. He had shown he was good enough to play for the Cats. Now it was time to see what he could do on the biggest stage of all. It was time for the championship.

***

Henry's first championship match was against Laois, who Kilkenny beat easily. Henry scored a massive 10 points, but DJ was the star of the show with two goals and three points. The two of them were forming quite a partnership up front. The master and the apprentice.

Next up was a much stiffer challenge. Offaly in the Leinster final.

'This is another step up, Henry,' warned big defender Pat O'Neill before the game. 'It won't be a day for tricks and flicks.'

The hits came hard and fast, but DJ and Henry were too hot to handle once more. DJ chipped in two goals and three points, and Henry slotted over six perfect points and scored a goal for good measure.

Can anyone stop the deadly duo?

Kilkenny won by 10 points. Henry was a Leinster champion at the age of just 19. To make it even better, he was named man of the match. He was walking on air!

He met his mam and dad after the game.

'Well done, Henry! We're so proud of you!' said his mam as she smothered him with a hug and gave him a big kiss.

'Thanks, Mam,' replied Henry, wiping his face. He was a bit embarrassed in front of all the lads!

'Good man, Henry. Knew you could do it! Some game!' his dad joined in.

Things were getting serious now. Kilkenny had a long break until their next game. Clare in the All-Ireland semi-final. Henry was wound up for the game. Too wound up, it turned out.

Clare were a rough, tough team and Henry came in for some heavy treatment. The great back Brian Lohan was making his life difficult, pucking him in the ribs every chance he got. Henry struggled and managed only three points all game. The Cats were getting bullied and they were behind in the closing stages. But once again, the great DJ came up trumps. A high ball was lofted into the square. Henry jumped for it but Lohan was right on top of him. The ball fell to the ground and broke for DJ. He only needed one chance. Seconds later, he whipped it high into the net.

Goooooal!

Kilkenny held on to win.

'You saved us, DJ!' said Henry with relief at the final whistle.

'That's what teammates do, Sheff,' replied DJ. 'We all have off days. You'll learn over the years. The more you play, the easier it gets.'

Now Kilkenny were into the All-Ireland final. Henry was having a dream first year. He thought nothing could go wrong.

They came face to face with the mighty Cork in the final, ending the season as they started. Henry scored five points and with less than twenty minutes to go Kilkenny were four points ahead. Henry thought they had it in the bag. But Cork had other ideas. They fired point after point and there was nothing Henry and his teammates could do to stop them. Henry could only stand and watch. It felt like a bad dream, but it was really happening. Cork had come back from the dead. The final whistle blew and Henry collapsed to the ground. His dream season had ended in defeat on the biggest stage of all, Croke Park.

Tears filled his eyes. He was so upset he could hardly bring himself to watch the Cork captain lift the Liam McCarthy Cup.

Cody came over and put his arm around Henry.

'Chin up, Henry! You can be very proud of how you played this year. You'll have plenty of big days ahead. We're going to have some great success together. I'm telling you.'

Henry couldn't bring himself to respond. He just stared into the distance. But he was already thinking of the future. He never wanted to feel like this again. He promised himself that next year he would be even better.

Chapter 12

All Star

Henry was angry all through the winter. The hurt of losing the All-Ireland final stayed with him. But in some ways it helped him focus. He knew he had to get better. He had shown he was ready to play at the highest level. He had great talent, everybody could see that. But he knew he had more inside him.

He was still young and found playing senior hurling tough. He was coming up against big men who were as hard as nails. He didn't like the physical battles. He liked to show off his skills. But he learned that at senior level you have to earn the right to play. You have to win the physical fight first. That was the big difference.

He talked to his dad and his older brothers. He always turned to them when he needed advice.

'You have all the talent, Henry,' Tommy told him. 'But that's no good to you if you don't do the work.'

'He's right, Henry,' said his dad. 'Look at what the top lads are at. The likes of DJ. And it's not just sport. You have to work hard at anything you want to do in life. Success won't just be handed to you. You have to work for it.'

They all agreed. Henry needed to toughen up. He needed to get bigger and stronger. Leaner and fitter. Stronger and faster. He needed to grow from a boy to a man.

Henry was always good at training on the field. But now he started to live like a proper athlete away from the pitch too. That meant no more trips to the chipper on a Saturday evening. No more fry-ups on the morning of a game. He started to eat all the right food. No crisps, cake or chocolate. He started running more and going to the gym. Nothing was going to stop him becoming one of the greats of the game. He had all the talent. Now he was putting the work in too.

***

By the time the summer came round he was fit as a fiddle and in fine form for the championship.

First up was Dublin in Croke Park. They were a team on the up and Kilkenny had to be on their toes. It wasn't just Henry who didn't want a repeat of last year. The whole Kilkenny team were raring to go. As a group they had trained harder than ever. Cody was in his second year as manager and the squad was coming together nicely. They meant business. And Dublin were about to be on the receiving end of their new-found determination.

From start to finish Kilkenny taught the Dubs a hurling lesson. The Cats had more skill, strength and style. And Henry was at the heart of it.

The first goal flew in after just 18 minutes. By half-time Kilkenny were ahead by 2-10 to 6 points. DJ was tormenting the Dublin defence. Henry was in sizzling form, enjoying the freedom of Croke Park. His shooting from frees and from play was even sharper than last year and he finished the game with six points.

Shefflin with another fine point! Desperate Dublin have nowhere to turn!

The Dubs didn't score a single point for most of the second half. Kilkenny won by 3-16 to 10 points. A thumping. But there was no big celebration.

'Good job, lads. But it's only beginning. Don't get carried away,' said Cody in the dressing room afterwards.

Now all eyes were on Offaly and the Leinster final.

Offaly were a little more competitive than Dublin, but not by much. It didn't seem possible, but Kilkenny went up another gear, and the game was over as a contest after 29 minutes when DJ found the back of the net. He sprinted away from his marker and thundered towards goal. Quick as a flash he ripped a rasping shot from the base of his hurl.

Goooooal!

'Yes, DJ!' roared Henry.

Henry added six points of his own as Kilkenny ran out easy winners. The deadly duo had done it again and Kilkenny were Leinster champions. But victory came at a cost to Henry. He hurt his shoulder and had to come off before the end. He was worried he might miss the All-Ireland semi-final.

After some rest and recovery he was back in action, ready to face Galway to battle for a place in the final. Galway had won the league and were unbeaten all season. They had greats like Eugene Cloonan and Ollie Canning in their team. This would be Kilkenny's toughest match of the year and there would be no room to hide. It was time for Henry to show that all his hard work over the winter was worth it.

It was a tight, tense and bruising contest. Galway matched Kilkenny in every department in the first half. It was a real battle between two equal teams. On 26 minutes Henry had a golden opportunity to put the Cats in control. He was slipped into space and had a clear sight of goal. He cracked off an instinctive shot and watched as it flew towards the top corner. Henry was sure it was going in. He thought it was perfect. But a Galway hurl got the slightest touch and it fizzed wide. Henry put his head in his hands.

Kilkenny had the better of the second half. Their defence tightened up and Henry, DJ and the rest of the forwards started to grow in confidence.

Shefflin the marksman finds his target again!

Henry added seven points as Kilkenny roared to victory. The final whistle blew and the game was over. Kilkenny were into another All-Ireland final. There were 42,000 fans in Croke Park that day and the half in Kilkenny's black and amber were going wild with excitement.

But Henry wasn't celebrating. He felt more relief than excitement. His only focus was the final now. They simply had to win.

Offaly were their opponents once more on a sunny day at Croke Park for the final. More than 60,000 fans made the trip for the big day on the second Sunday in September. The green, white and gold of Offaly and the black and amber of Kilkenny turned the stadium into a festival of colour. But deep down inside the stadium, away from all the fans, there was only one thing on Henry's mind. Winning.

Cody asked him to say a few words to the team. Henry wasn't used to speaking in the dressing room. He was still young and wasn't considered one of the team's leaders. But he made a powerful speech.

'I remember the pain of losing last year,' he said as his teammates stood around him in a circle, their arms linked around each other's shoulders.

'I never want to feel like that again. I've worked too hard over the winter to let this slip now. We all did. We're not losing today,' he said emotionally.

'I've done all I can now,' said Cody calmly as the referee knocked on the door to call them onto the field. 'It's up to you now, lads.'

With Henry's words ringing in their ears, Kilkenny charged into action. Offaly hadn't a hope.

Henry, wearing his green helmet, with number 12 on his back, was on fire from the start. He set up DJ for the opening goal.

Goooooal!

Minutes later Henry was free again.

Henry bearing in on goal. Stopped on the line!

Henry's shot was stopped before the ball trickled over the line. DJ ran in to smash it into the net.

It's in!

'That's my goal!' roared Henry.

'No way,' laughed DJ. 'I got the last touch!'

Henry was annoyed. He saw the umpire raising the green flag before DJ even touched it.

There was only one way to make up for it, he thought to himself. Score another.

His chance came in the second half.

Everything is going right for Kilkenny. Can they get another? Henry's innnnnnn! Henry's scoooorrreeddddd!

'Yesssss!' Henry leapt into the air.

'You're not taking this one off me, DJ!' he shouted over the roar of the Kilkenny fans.

It was a day when everything went right for Kilkenny. They scored a remarkable five goals on their way to a huge win.

Kilkenny have won the first hurling final of the new millennium!

Kilkenny were back where they belonged. The hurt of last year was over. They were the All-Ireland champions for the 26th time. But it was Henry's first. A special moment. He danced a jig on the podium as he lifted the Liam McCarthy Cup high into the sky. All the sacrifice was worth it for this one taste of glory.

Chapter 13

Becoming a Star

Henry enjoyed himself over the winter. A little too much. He had worked hard for his All-Ireland success and he wanted to make the most of it. He was enjoying college life in Waterford. He was studying business, but as always, hurling was more important to him.

The college had a great team, with players like Éamonn Corcoran from Tipperary, Andy Moloney from Waterford and Alan Geoghegan from Kilkenny. They became great friends. But there wasn't much study done between the hurling, nights out and playing pranks on each other.

With all the craic, Henry started to take his eye off the ball a little. He had forgotten the good habits that brought him success the year before. He had become a bit too full of himself. He thought he was the man and that success would always come easily. But he was wrong.

Kilkenny started the league well enough. Henry was in good form. He hit a goal and five points in an opening win against Laois. Then another goal against Waterford. But the first sign that everything wasn't right came in the next game against old enemies Cork. Henry could manage only five points and Kilkenny lost the game. Next up he scored 1–4 in a draw with Tipperary. Kilkenny looked a long way from the team that won the All-Ireland just last summer. Their league campaign soon came to an abrupt end.

They put their disappointment behind them. Now it was time to focus on the All-Ireland.

Kilkenny's first match was against Offaly. Henry had a fine game, finishing with a goal and six points. Then they hammered Wexford in the Leinster final. Henry scored another four points. But that was as good as it would get that year.

In the All-Ireland quarter-final they were ambushed by Galway. Kilkenny were no match for them. They were simply blown away. Henry managed nine points, but the Cats just couldn't keep up. Galway forward Eugene Cloonan put Henry in the shade with an incredible two goals and nine points. Kilkenny's dressing room was completely silent after the game. They had gone from All-Ireland champions to crashing out early in the quarter-finals. It was a year to forget.

The defeat was a wake-up call for all of them. Just like Henry, the whole squad had gone soft. They celebrated their win the previous year too much. They forgot the lesson that talent brings success only if you work hard too. They were in for a difficult winter.

The first night back at training the following season Cody read them the riot act.

'Think back to the day we played Galway last summer.' He was red in the face but he wasn't shouting. It reminded Henry of when his parents were angry. You always knew you were in more trouble when they went quiet. It was easier when they shouted.

'There was too much craic before the game,' Cody went on. 'You were all too relaxed. You thought you had the game won before you even played it.'

Cody was tearing strips off the players. And they knew he was right. Henry picked a spot on the ground and stared at it. Cody was fierce when he was in this kind of mood.

'And you, Henry!' Cody singled him out.

'Oh no!' thought Henry. 'I'm in for it now.'

'You've gone soft. You think success is going to be handed to you. Nobody gets success in this game without putting in the work. You're a shadow of the player you were two years ago.'

The harsh words stung Henry. But that's exactly what Cody wanted. He wanted a reaction. Deep down inside, Henry knew Cody was right. He wasn't working as hard as he could. He hadn't kicked on from his glorious first season. He knew if he didn't pull up his socks, Cody would drop him. All he ever wanted was to play for Kilkenny and he wasn't going to let it slip now. So, not for the first time, he decided to make the changes he needed to.

He was in his final year in college now, so he knuckled down to his studies. The nights out were over. The craic with the lads had to stop. He took a job as a labourer on building sites, lifting blocks and mixing cement, to help toughen him up. He started walking everywhere to boost his fitness and lose some weight. He watched what he ate even more than ever. He trained harder than ever. There was no looking back now. By the time the first match came around, Henry was a different beast. He was ready for action. He was about to become a superstar.

Their first match of the summer was against Offaly. Cody called Henry over before the throw-in.

'This is it, Henry. You've done everything we asked of you. You've done the hard work. Go out and show them what you can do. It's time to shine.'

Henry felt 10 feet tall. Cody's simple words had worked their magic. He charged onto the pitch and never looked back. Everything he hit that day went over the bar.

Shefflin! Straight between the posts!

Henry sticks another one!

Majestic! A hurling masterclass!

'You're on fire, Sheff,' shouted his strike partner Eddie Brennan, who scored a goal himself.

'You're not doin' too bad yourself, Eddie!' Henry laughed back.

Henry scored 11 points that day, seven from play. Kilkenny won well and Henry was walking on air.

The Cats were made to work much harder in the Leinster final against Wexford. It was a much tougher match, but Henry still managed to make his mark. He scored eight points and

Kilkenny scraped a win by just two points. They were Leinster champions again, but this year was all about the All-Ireland. The Cats and Henry weren't finished yet.

They were up against Tipperary in the All-Ireland semi-final. Henry would be directly marked by Éamonn Corcoran, his best friend from college. He always found it weird when his friend became a rival. But for 70 minutes on the pitch their friendship was set aside. Friends or not, they were both out to win.

It was an epic game. Henry and Corcoran tore strips off each other. Nobody watching would have known they were friends. At half-time it was all to play for. DJ made a stirring speech in the dressing room.

'We've all worked too hard for this. We're not losing today!' he roared, banging his hurl on the table.

Henry was playing at centre-forward and scored eight crucial points. But it was a spark of genius from DJ that would win the game. He picked up possession and flicked a lightning-fast handpass to Jimmy Coogan. The Tipperary backs didn't even see where the sliotar had gone, it moved so quickly. Jimmy took aim and fired.

Goooooal!

'DJ, you're a genius!' Henry shouted as he jumped for joy.

'It was me who scored!' laughed Jimmy.

The goal was enough to win the game. Kilkenny were into the All-Ireland final once more. This time Clare were the opponents.

There wasn't much talk in the Croke Park dressing room before the big game. Everyone on the Kilkenny team knew what they had to do. Cody's team talk was short. Henry simply nodded at DJ in the tunnel. No words were needed.

On the pitch, Kilkenny simply blew Clare away. It was an exhibition of hurling and Henry was the artist. He had the freedom of the pitch and seemed to score whenever he wanted to.

Just three minutes in he won a high ball in the air and flicked it down to DJ.

Goooooal!

The deadly double act was just warming up.

A few minutes later Henry was in again and whipped a high shot at goal.

What a save! Davy keeps Clare in it!

Clare's Davy Fitzgerald was one of the best goalkeepers in the game. He was almost impossible to beat. And he loved a bit of banter on the pitch too.

'Did you like that, Henry? You'll have to do better than that to beat me!' he roared.

Henry turned and walked away. But he was steaming inside.

Clare fought hard but they were no match for Kilkenny. Henry scored point after point to the roars of the 76,000-strong crowd. Henry knew the game was won by now but he wanted a goal to crown his incredible performance. Just before the end he got his chance.

Swept inside! Dangerous ball!

Sheffffllllllinnnnnnnn!

Goooooal!

That's secured the title for the Cats!

Henry's perfect flick nestled in the bottom corner. He couldn't resist a dig at Davy.

'That'll keep you quiet!' he roared at the Clare goalkeeper.

The referee finally blew the whistle. Kilkenny had won the cup. Henry had to pinch himself. He finished with 1-7, DJ with 1-6. He thought it couldn't get much better. All-Ireland champions and a goal in the final. It was more than he ever dreamed of. But it got better still. He was named man of the match and then player of the year. His prize was a brand-new car! Not bad for a young lad who had just finished college. Henry was now recognised as the best player in the whole country. He could hardly believe it. A rainbow emerged in the sky above Croke Park as the celebrations went on. Henry took a moment to himself and looked up. He had his own crock of gold in his hands. The Liam McCarthy Cup.

Chapter 14

A Year to Forget

Kilkenny won another All-Ireland the following year with a three-point win over their old enemy Cork. DJ had laid out the path to victory in the dressing room.

'Get the ball in and we'll score goals!' he told his teammates. And that's exactly what they did. It was DJ's last game for Kilkenny. His sparkling career had come to an end. He was one of the all-time greats. But Henry showed there was life after DJ for Kilkenny. He was in top form in the final, scoring six points and was named on the All Star team once more. On the pitch, everything was rosy. Away from hurling, things were going nicely too.

Henry met the girl of his dreams that winter. Her name was Deirdre and she was Miss Kilkenny. Henry thought she was beautiful the minute he laid eyes on her. She noticed him too, but didn't know he was a famous Kilkenny hurler until her sister told her. She was a camogie player as well, which was a bonus! They started to go out together and soon fell in love. Everyone was so happy for them. Except Deirdre's father. He was a huge Kilkenny hurling fan and was worried that Henry might be distracted from the game.

'Stay away from Henry!' he joked to Deirdre. 'He has a busy year ahead of him!'

Henry had finished college and started working in his first job. He was a salesman for a pharmaceutical company. He was loving life. But he didn't know that the glory days were about to come to an end quickly. In sport, and in life, the moment you think everything is going right is exactly the moment it starts to go wrong.

The season started with a big shock. Kilkenny lost to Wexford. It was their first defeat in Leinster in seven years. They were struggling without DJ. Cody was so angry afterwards. Henry knew he was right. They had let their guard down and were caught out. That meant they went into the qualifiers for the first time, facing a dangerous Galway team.

But this time it was different. Henry knew he had to step into DJ's shoes. It was his turn to lead the team now. And, true to form, he had one of the games of his life. One of those rare moments when everything went right. He scored two goals and 11 points. The Cats hammered Galway. Henry was untouchable. But that was as good as it got for him that year.

Next up they faced Clare in the All-Ireland quarter-final. Henry was hoping for another big performance. But everything changed in an instant. He jumped for a ball and took a heavy blow from a hurl across his face. It whacked his eye.

Owwwwwwwwwwww!

'I can't see!' Henry roared with panic in his voice. He lay on the ground in pain and frightened. The doctor came on and knew it didn't look good. The stretcher was brought on and as he was taken off the pitch Henry started crying. Just like when he was a teenager, he had badly hurt his eye again. He was rushed to hospital with a garda escort.

The doctor took a look and did some tests. He said Henry had torn his tear duct. It was a serious injury, but he was lucky. A millimetre closer and he could have lost his eye. Nobody expected him to play again for the rest of the year. But, Henry being Henry, he was determined to get back as quickly as he could. He found out in hospital that Kilkenny had won the match. And now he wanted to be back for the semi-final. Everybody thought it was a big mistake!

His eyesight started to get better by the middle of the week, and by the following Sunday he was back on the pitch. It was an amazing recovery. What's more, after just a few minutes against Waterford he heard the familiar sound of the sliotar hitting the back of the net.

Goooooal!

Later he added another one for good measure. Kilkenny were back in an All-Ireland final once more. Everybody was talking about Henry and his amazing recovery.

Henry's vision had come back, but it was a long time before he felt brave enough to go up for a high ball again. He was still nervous and it was affecting his performance on the pitch.

Kilkenny were up against their great rivals Cork again in the final. This time the Cats were nowhere near good enough. Cork were out for revenge and they got it in style. Henry scored five points, but he wasn't up to his usual standard. None of the Kilkenny team was, and in truth they were hammered. It sickened

Henry to see the Cork players celebrate on the pitch. He really didn't like the sight of that red jersey.

The following season was worse again. It seemed Kilkenny and Henry had lost their magic touch. They were dumped out of the All-Ireland by Galway. Everybody was saying that the Cats were finished and it was time for Cody to move on. Henry was feeling the pressure.

To make matters worse, things weren't much better off the pitch either. Henry didn't like his new job. He was spending long hours driving. It affected his diet and training and he started to lose too much weight. He wasn't happy in his hurling and he wasn't happy with his job. It was a nightmare. But he kept all the bad feelings inside, not telling anybody how he felt. It was all becoming too much for him. He was finding it hard to handle the pressure.

He decided to pay a visit to Cody for a chat. He wanted to tell him everything that was on his mind. Being the great manager that he is, Cody was happy to listen. They talked for hours. The pair had a great heart-to-heart and Henry laid out everything that was on his mind. His disappointment at how his hurling was going, his struggles away from the pitch.

'I'm going nowhere,' Cody told Henry. 'I know exactly how to get us back to the top. We have to rebuild a new team now that DJ is gone. Bring through some new faces. I want you to be our leader. The main man. But first there's something I want you to do for me. You need a break from the game. It's not so much your body but your mind. I'm going to leave you out of the squad for the league next year. But I want you back for the championship. I want you fit and firing and ready to go.'

'No problem, boss. Sounds like a plan!' Henry agreed.

He instantly felt better. It's always good to talk when there's something on your mind.

Henry used the break over the winter to start building his own house on land his dad owned back in Ballyhale. He dug the foundations himself, with his brother John laying the bricks and some of his teammates helping too. A real family and community effort.

There was only one more job he had to do now before the end of the year. He went away for a weekend with Deirdre. And he plucked up the courage to ask her to marry him. She said yes! The perfect way to end what had been a bad year.

Chapter 15

Back in Business

Now that everything was in place off the pitch, it was time for Henry to get back to business on it. He enjoyed his break over the winter and was ready to return to action. Kilkenny had done well in the league without him and had made it to the semi-finals. They were up against Tipperary once more. The perfect game for Henry's comeback. And he wasted no time showing everyone what they had been missing.

Goooooal! Henry strikes again!

He scored 1-3 in total as Kilkenny saw off Tipp to reach the league final. Henry was happy but more relieved to be back in action. He still felt a bit rusty but knew he would improve with more games. And how right he was.

The final against Limerick was played at Semple Stadium in Thurles. Henry was at his best right from the start. Catching a high ball and swerving to score a sublime point over his shoulder. The crowd gasped in amazement.

Wowwwwww!

But there was more to come. Soon Henry found the back of the net. Eoin Larkin went on a surging run through the middle and handpassed to Henry, who scooped the sliotar high with his first touch and calmly poked it past the goalkeeper with his second.

Goooooal! That's Kilkenny for you! Who else but Henry!

He scored another before the end, finishing with two goals and six points as Kilkenny claimed the league title. But they didn't celebrate too much. In the dressing room afterwards, Cody was quick to remind them that bigger challenges lay ahead.

'Well done, boys. Good stuff!' he said. But he wasn't exactly full of praise. 'There's plenty more to work on. This is just the start. We'll need to be better if we're going to stop Cork in the All-Ireland.'

For everyone in Kilkenny there was just one thing on their mind that year. Stopping Cork winning three All-Irelands in a row. While the Cats were away, Cork were at play. They won the last two All-Irelands and were being talked about as one of the best teams ever, with the great goalkeeper Dónal Óg Cusack, Seán Óg Ó hAilpín, and 'The Rock' Diarmuid O'Sullivan. Henry still remembered watching them dancing on the Croke Park pitch in celebration. Something he never wanted to see again.

Kilkenny blitzed through the Leinster Championship. They thumped Westmeath, with Henry scoring eight points. Then Wexford wilted as Henry notched another goal and seven points. He was on fire. Maybe Kilkenny weren't finished after all. With Henry in this kind of form, anything was possible.

The Cats were drawn to face Galway in the quarter-finals. A great chance to make up for last year's defeat. Henry wanted revenge and he showed it. He started at full-forward but went out to half-forward in search of more ball. And it paid off.

Henry hits another! It's like he has a laser target guiding the ball over the bar!

He finished with 11 points as Kilkenny came through an exciting game. The season was building nicely and Henry was back on top form. Kilkenny were now into the semi-final to face Clare. Cork were on the other side of the draw, and they would play Waterford. Almost everyone in the country wanted to see a Cork/ Kilkenny final. Henry most of all. He dreamed of the chance.

Henry went up another level in the game against Clare. Starting as he meant to go on after just one minute.

The first test for the Clare defence ... Shefflin ... Goooooal! A spectacular start by Kilkenny!

Henry was roaming all over the forward line and it seemed that every time he touched the ball he scored. Whether in the air, on the ground, or stuck in a swirl of defenders, Henry had the skills to beat any defender. The Clare defenders were left with headaches trying to track him. In the end he scored an amazing goal and 13 points. It was one of the best ever performances in the black and amber shirt. He had now scored 2-38 in just four games. Nobody had seen the likes of it before.

But Henry and the rest of the Kilkenny team didn't celebrate. They were focused on the one thing they wanted. Stopping Cork winning three in a row. Word came in that Cork had beaten Waterford in the other semi-final. The stage was set. It was the final everyone wanted. The great Cork going for a famous three in a row. The comeback Cats, with Henry right back in form, gunning to stop them.

It was Henry's fifth All-Ireland final. But after winning nothing for two years, this final felt like the most important one yet. The dressing room was tense before the game. Every Kilkenny player was focused on the task in hand. Cody laid out the instructions on the blackboard. But today wasn't a day for tactics.

'Hurling is a simple game, lads,' Cody said in his typical plain way. 'You know what to do.'

Henry joined in. 'Remember the pain of the last two years!' he roared as the players were about to go onto the pitch. 'I don't want to see those Cork lads celebrating in front of us again. We're winning today!' He thumped his fist into his hand.

He hardly needed to say anything. Every one of the Kilkenny team was as pumped as he was.

It was a glorious sunny day at Croke Park. The stage was set for one of the most intense finals ever played. As soon as the ball was thrown in, Kilkenny smashed everything in red that moved. Tactics went out of the window.

It was blood and guts now. The team that wanted it most would win. Cork didn't take a step back. They weren't two-time champions for nothing. It was a battle royal!

The teams were level five times in the first half hour. There was nothing to separate them. Then came the moment of the match. The ball broke to Aidan Fogarty, the young Kilkenny forward playing in his first final. And quick as a flash he let rip.

A goooooal! Aidan Fogarty! Kilkenny fans are overjoyed!

'Yes!' shouted Henry as he ran over to celebrate. 'That's the stuff!'

It was enough to put them ahead at the break. Henry kept the scoreboard ticking over, accurate as ever from frees. But Cork weren't going to lie down. With just four minutes to play, they were right back in the match.

McCarthy ... finds O'Connor ... Ben O'Connor strikes it ...

Goooooal!

It's not over yet! What a game!

'Don't panic, lads. Keep the heads and keep going!' shouted Henry, trying to calm his teammates. But he knew they were hanging on.

The closing stages were unbearable. Kilkenny were standing tough as Cork pushed for a goal. Cody was pacing up and down on the touchline. Henry was running his legs into the ground until he had no more to give. His body was begging for the game to end. And just when he thought he could give no more he heard the sweet sound of the referee's whistle. *Peep ... peep ... peeeeeeep!*

It's all over!

Kilkenny are the All-Ireland champions!

The Rebel Treble comes to an end. The Cats are back!

Henry stood still and looked up to the skies. He could hardly believe it. Cody ran onto the pitch and grabbed Henry for a big hug. The two of them stood arm in arm, almost in tears. They had done it together. A journey that all started with a chat between the two men that set everything straight.

Kilkenny were back on top. And Henry was the player of the year once more.

Chapter 16

Pride of the Parish

Winning a fourth All-Ireland with Kilkenny still wasn't enough for Henry. Not this year anyway. He wanted more. In the days after victory over Cork, while everyone was celebrating, Henry was already thinking about his next big game. He wanted the taste of success again. But this time with his local club Ballyhale. Winning the club All-Ireland title, with his friends and family there beside him, would be more than special. He wanted to do it for the pride of the parish.

When Henry was growing up, Ballyhale had been the best club team in the country. By the time he was 10, they had won three club All-Irelands, a remarkable achievement for a village with little more than a hundred houses. Hurling was everything in Ballyhale and watching the teams of his childhood winning everything was the reason Henry took up the game in the first place.

But the team hadn't been good for a long time now. It was 15 years since they had won a county title. Henry felt he could help inspire the next generation. Give the children of Ballyhale a new set of heroes to cheer. The best way to do that, he thought, was to become All-Ireland champions once more. To do that they first had to win the Kilkenny club championship. No pressure!

Henry knew they had a good team that year. But more important, they had a great bond. They were a band of brothers. Henry's brother Paul was in the full-back line. His old schoolmates from St Patrick's, Bob Aylward and Aidan Cummins, were there too. So were the Reid brothers, TJ, Eoin and Patrick, along with Mark Aylward, Michael Fennelly and James 'Cha' Fitzpatrick. All great players and even better friends.

They needed to draw on that team spirit right at the start of the season when Ballyhale found themselves nine points down to Carrickshock. But Henry told his teammates not to panic. And sure enough, he came to their rescue, scoring five points from play in a fine comeback. They were up and running.

In the semi-final they beat Dunnamaggin. Now they were in the final against age-old rivals O'Loughlin Gaels. The final was played on a cold November day in Nowlan Park. But there was plenty of heat in the battle. Ballyhale needed Henry to be at his best and he didn't let them down. He scored 10 points in a tough win. Mark Aylward scored a goal and two points, TJ Reid another three, Cha Fitzpatrick three more, Patrick Reid two, while Michael Fennelly and Aidan Cummins chipped in with a point each. It was a mighty team effort. Henry was jumping for joy. It was one of his most memorable days on the hurling field. Ballyhale were champions of Kilkenny after a 15-year wait. Henry and his teammates had their hands on the Tom Walsh Cup. The celebrations were wild. People cried with delight in the village that night. Henry was the talk of the village. Just as he dreamed he would be when he was a little boy working behind the counter in Sheffs.

But the journey wasn't over yet. Now they had to play the best in Leinster. Just a week later they were back on the pitch against Rathnure from Wexford. They didn't have the ideal preparation for the game with all the celebrating the week before. But Henry was bang on form again, smashing home a goal and three points in a seven-point win.

Now to face Birr in the Leinster final.

Birr had long been big rivals of Ballyhale back in their golden era. There was always talk of them in the village when Henry was growing up. They were the most successful club in

Ireland and Henry and his teammates knew they were in for a real battle. But they were starting to click. Everything was falling into place and Henry began to dream that it might be their year to go all the way. The scoreboard was a familiar sight again. Reids, Aylwards, Fitzpatricks and, top of the pile, Henry Shefflin. He scored another goal and five points. Ballyhale were Leinster champions.

Just two more games to go now and this tiny village in the heart of Kilkenny could be the All-Ireland champions. Henry dared to dream.

If their comeback in the first round against Carrickshock was memorable, the All-Ireland semi-final against Toomevara from Tipperary was another thing entirely. Ballyhale needed every last bit of their team spirit to come through this one. At one stage they were 12 points behind.

Surely there's no way back for Ballyhale now!

But with Henry in their team there was always hope. Just before the break, Patrick Reid scrambled home a goal. Henry kept knocking over free after free. And soon they were back in the game. TJ slipped over a sublime sideline cut. Next Henry set up a chance for Cha.

Shefflin slides it to Fitzpatrick ...

Goooooal!

'Yes, Cha!' roared Henry. 'Keep it going!'

Next Bob Aylward smashed over a long-range point. They were ahead now and weren't going to let go. Cha added another point and Henry finished the scoring with his seventh free. They had done it! A huge comeback. Henry puffed out his cheeks with relief. They were off to Croke Park for the All-Ireland final on St Patrick's Day.

'Is this real?' said Henry as he hugged Bob and Cha.

'We don't make it easy!' laughed Bob. 'Sure, where's the fun in that?'

The village was decorated in the club colours of green and white for the week leading up to the final. Every window, lamp post and car had a flag flying. Good luck signs lined the road. This was one of the biggest days ever in Ballyhale. The entire village travelled to Croke Park for the final against Loughrea from Galway.

Henry was well used to the stadium from all the matches he played with Kilkenny. But for some of his teammates it was their first time playing at the famous ground. Henry looked round the dressing room. For all his glory with Kilkenny, this was different. He was togging out for an All-Ireland final, but this time his brother was beside him. His best friends from school. His family friends from around Ballyhale. It was special.

They gathered in a circle with their arms around each other.

'When I was a small boy,' Henry said, almost choking up, 'I only ever dreamed of playing for Ballyhale. Kilkenny was never even on my mind. Here we are now together. In Croke Park on All-Ireland final day. Take in every moment of this. We might never be here again. Don't let the game pass you by.'

Henry's speech made the players feel unbeatable. They felt the history of the club. The pride of the parish. There was no way they were losing this one.

'Come on, Ballyhale!' roared Cha.

Loughrea were a tough team. They made a plan to keep Henry quiet. Every time he moved he was hit, blocked or hooked. He wasn't able to have his usual impact on the game. But while Loughrea did everything to stop Henry, they didn't plan for the deadly Reid brothers. While Henry was kept quiet, they came up with the goods.

Goooooal!

Goooooal!

Goooooal!

Together they scored three goals and seven points. TJ, Eoin and Patrick were the stars of Croke Park. Henry added three points too in a seven-point win. He was walking on air when the final whistle blew.

Ballyhale are the All-Ireland club champions! King Henry has done it again!

Henry ran straight to his brother Paul for a huge hug. His brother John, who was a selector, soon caught up with them. Then Cha jumped on board, Bob Aylward and Aidan Cummins too for good measure. The Reid brothers piled on as the fans started to charge towards them. Soon half the village of Ballyhale was in the middle of the pitch in Croke Park in a huge group hug. Henry was right at the heart of it, with tears in his eyes. In that moment, he thought, he would swap everything he had ever won with Kilkenny, the All-Irelands, All Stars and Player of the Year Awards, just for this one moment. It was pure magic. The pride of the parish.

Chapter 17

Pure Glory

Henry was made captain of Kilkenny for the following season. Cody called him soon after the club All-Ireland final.

'You've done your bit for Ballyhale,' he said bluntly. 'The work starts with Kilkenny again now.'

It was a huge honour for Henry. And he was determined to be a successful captain.

Kilkenny picked up exactly where they left off the year before. In their first match of the championship they opened up Offaly. Henry scored 12 points.

He's a joy to watch!

Then they wiped the floor with Wexford. Another nine points for Henry.

He's a master of his craft!

They gutted Galway in the All-Ireland quarter-final. Henry scored eight more frees.

He never misses!

They whipped Wexford once more in the semi-final.

A fabulous 14 points for Henry!

Everything was going right for Henry, and Kilkenny had sailed into another All-Ireland final. This time against Limerick.

Limerick didn't know what hit them in the early stages of the final. Henry and the rest of his teammates were well up for the game. Henry flew into an early challenge with a strong shoulder. Eddie Brennan scored a goal after just a few minutes.

'Yes, Eddie! Magic!' said Henry, pumping his fist.

Now it was his turn. Just a minute later, Cha got the ball in space and found Henry on the edge of the square. The deadly Ballyhale double act were teaming up again, this time in the black and amber of Kilkenny. Henry didn't even think about what he was going to do. Whoooooshhhhhh!

Goooooal! Two in two minutes. Limerick are shellshocked!

Just 10 minutes in and Kilkenny already had one hand on the cup. Henry felt he had the freedom of Croke Park and was enjoying every second. When suddenly disaster struck.

Owwwwwwwwwww!

He went into a challenge and took a heavy knock to his knee. He felt something pop. It wasn't good. He bravely tried to play on, but he couldn't. His knee was gone. He could hardly walk, never mind run. He went in at half-time and the doctor told him his day was over. It was a serious ligament injury. Not only would he miss the second half, he would be out for the best part of a year. He burst into tears.

The rest of the Kilkenny players promised to finish the job and win the cup for Henry. And that's what they did, wrapping up a seven-point win. Henry was heartbroken that his day ended early but still overjoyed that he had captained Kilkenny to All-Ireland glory. He hobbled up the steps to lift the Liam McCarthy Cup.

A few days later he had another night to remember. Even though he was in serious pain, nothing would stop him joining in the celebrations as he brought the famous cup back home to Ballyhale.

***

He had a long winter trying to get his knee better. After surgery, he had to do loads of boring exercises to make it strong again. He spent hours in the swimming pool jogging from one side to the other in the shallow end. He hated being away from the hurling field and the craic with the lads, but he knew what he had to do.

He missed the league entirely. But by the following summer he was just about ready for action again. He wore a big bandage on his knee for Kilkenny's first match of the championship against Offaly. He felt stiff and off the pace, but he managed to score 11 points and set up a goal. Not a bad way to make a comeback.

He scored another goal and seven points against Wexford in the Leinster final. He was scoring at least, but he still didn't feel he was giving everything to the team. He wasn't getting stuck in like before. He was afraid to tackle. He was worried he would hurt his knee again.

Kilkenny came up against old rivals Cork in the All-Ireland semi-final. Henry knew this was another step up. Kilkenny had yet to be really tested, and people were saying Henry wasn't the same player since his knee injury. At times, he believed it himself.

As ever, it was a ferocious contest. Even for a match between Cork and Kilkenny this was something special. Every time the Cats scored, the Rebels bounced back. The tackles flew in, the points flew over. The crowd gasped. It was one of the fastest games of hurling ever seen. Suddenly Eoin Larkin fizzed home a ferocious shot.

Goooooal! Kilkenny are ahead in this rip-roaring contest!

For the first time in almost a year, Henry forgot about his knee. He flashed over a fine point early in the second half and raised his arm in the air. He felt good. He was back on form and back in the heart of the action, scoring nine points in a big win for Kilkenny. Any win over Cork was always special. For Henry, showing he was back to his best made it even better.

To make it sweeter still, Kilkenny were now going for three in a row themselves. If they did it, they would be the first team in more than 30 years to pull off this remarkable achievement. Their opponents in the final were Waterford. Kilkenny's neighbours and the county where

Henry was born. They didn't often go head to head in an All-Ireland final. So everyone expected fireworks. But Kilkenny had other ideas.

From the first whistle to the last, the Cats simply blew Waterford away. Henry and his teammates were in the zone. They couldn't miss. Eddie Brennan scored two goals. Henry hit nine points. Waterford were put to the sword. In a memorable moment, Henry caught a puckout right on his hurl, twirling around in mid-air like a ballerina. The crowd couldn't believe what they were seeing. Even Henry didn't know how he had done it.

'You're showing off now, Sheff!' laughed Eddie.

'Go away out of that!' Henry smiled back. If only every game was as easy as this.

In the end, Kilkenny won out by an amazing 23 points.

They've done it! Three in a row!

There was no doubting now that they were one of the greatest teams of all time.

As the fans jumped up and down and cheered, Henry thought to himself what a difference a year makes. From the sadness of getting injured last year, now he was back on top of the world.

Henry was named on the All Star team again. His sixth in a row! To make it even sweeter, his first daughter, Sadhbh, was born that year. He put her in the cup and stood for a photo alongside his wife, Deirdre. They were all laughing and Henry couldn't have been happier. On and off the field, everything was perfect.

Chapter 18

Tipperary Trilogy

Over the years Henry had enjoyed many battles on the field against fierce rivals. From coming up against James Stephens as a young boy playing with Ballyhale, to the great battles with Kilkenny against Galway and especially Cork. Now there was a new rival emerging. Tipperary.

They were a great hurling county. They didn't have much success for a while, but they had been getting better year by year under their new manager, Liam Sheedy. And they had some great players, like goalkeeper Brendan Cummins and star forwards Eoin Kelly and Lar Corbett. Now they faced their biggest test yet. An All-Ireland final against Kilkenny.

The Cats had continued their fine form throughout the year and were back once more for another big day in Croke Park. It was like a second home to them now. They were going for a historic four in a row. Something only one team had ever achieved before. The great Cork team way back in the 1940s. Henry knew he and his teammates would be considered legends for ever if they won this one. But Tipperary weren't going to make it easy.

Henry clipped on his green helmet and prepared for battle. The referee blew his whistle and the game was on. It was hot and heavy from the start. Henry had an early chance.

Whoosh!

Save!

A fine stop from Brendan Cummins!

Tipperary threw everything at Kilkenny. The Cats struck back blow for blow. At half-time Kilkenny were just two points ahead. Henry felt he hadn't been at his best. In the dressing room at the break, Cody asked the boys for more.

'Come on, Henry! We need you!' he said.

Those few simple words were just what Henry needed to hear. He doubled his efforts in the second half, in what became one of the most memorable games of hurling ever played.

The points fizzed over one after another. First Tipp, then Kilkenny. There was nothing between them. The hits were heavy and Henry was breathing hard. Suddenly, Tipp's Benny Dunne took a wild pull across Tommy Walsh.

Owwwwww!

He smashed him. The referee had no choice but to send him off.

Red card! Tipperary are down to 14 men!

Nobody likes to see a player sent off in an All-Ireland final. But Henry knew this was their chance. It was now or never.

'Come on, lads!' he roared. 'Keep blocking and hooking!'

But it wasn't happening for Kilkenny. They were still two points down with 10 minutes to go. Only for their goalkeeper, PJ Ryan, they would have been way behind. Then came a lifeline.

Richie Hogan burst forward for the Cats, fighting off his markers.

Peeeeeep! The referee's whistle blew.

It's a penalty! That looked very harsh!

The Tipperary players couldn't believe it. Henry knew right away the responsibility would fall on his shoulders. He picked up the sliotar and gathered his thoughts. This was it. The All-Ireland final on the line. One shot at glory.

As he faced the goal, his world started to close in. The fans were screaming, the referee was talking to him, the Tipp players were trying to put him off. He closed his eyes for a moment and thought back to when he was a boy. He pretended he was on the squash court behind his house. He remembered what his dad had told him. Pick your spot and don't change your mind. He thought of the penalty he took as a teenager for Ballyhale. But this time he wasn't going to miss. He opened his eyes and took a deep breath. The goal seemed to get smaller by the second. Here goes ...

Goooooal!

It's in the back of the net! Henry Shefflin saves the day for the Cats!

Henry felt sheer relief. He hadn't been at his best, but he showed guts when his team needed him most.

Seconds later, Martin Comerford smashed home a second goal for Kilkenny. It was in the bag now.

Goooooal!

Kilkenny have made history with another All-Ireland. Four in a row!

Henry was exhausted, battered and bruised. But as soon as the whistle went, the pain disappeared. The winning feeling rushed over him. He never tired of it. It seemed to taste sweeter every year.

They had won the battle. But the war against Tipperary wasn't over. They would be back the next year. Better than ever.

***

The following year, Henry reached another milestone in the early stages of the Leinster Championship. His fourth point against Dublin made him the highest-scoring player in the history of the All-Ireland hurling championship, overtaking the great Kilkenny player Eddie Keher. It was a special moment for him personally, but as always his main focus was on the team. And there were bigger days ahead.

Kilkenny marched into the All-Ireland semi-final where the familiar sight of the red jerseys of Cork awaited them. Early in the first half Henry felt a familiar pop in his knee.

Owwwwwww!

His old injury had come back. He had to come off, fighting back the tears once more. But even without Henry, Kilkenny were too strong for Cork. Henry was proud of his teammates but now he had just one thought in his mind. Getting back in time for the All-Ireland final in three weeks' time, where Tipperary were waiting for them once more.

Everybody thought it was impossible. Other players would be out for a year. But once again, Henry had other ideas. He did everything to make his knee better. He went to doctors and physios and got treatment from a specialist in Limerick. He even tried the latest technology, taking sessions in a freezing cold room to try to help the blood flow to his knee. It was miserable sitting in the freezing cold. But it was all worth it for the chance to make it back in time for the big match.

Henry's work paid off and he was able to train again a few days before the final. He wasn't really sure if his knee would hold up, but it was worth a crack. Against all odds, Henry was named to start in the team for the final. He had done the impossible. Nobody could believe it. It was all the talk in the build-up to the big match.

In the end, it was a step too far. Even for Henry. Just 13 minutes into the game his knee buckled under him. There was no pain this time. Just sadness. His All-Ireland final was over.

'Chin up, Henry!' said Cody as he walked off the pitch. 'At least you gave it a go!'

Without him, Kilkenny fell short against Tipperary. Henry could only watch on from the sidelines as Tipp won the day and stopped the Cats from winning five in a row.

Afterwards, many people were saying this was definitely the end of Henry Shefflin. He's starting to get a bit older, they said. Nobody comes back from two serious knee injuries. Maybe he's better off out of the game. But all the talk just made Henry smile. There was no way he was leaving the game like this. He knew he had a mountain to climb. But he knew he'd be back.

***

As it turned out, the final the next year was once more between Kilkenny and Tipperary.

The two best teams in the country came head to head again. Kilkenny had won the first meeting, Tipperary the second. Now it was time for the decider in this thrilling trilogy. The nation was gripped.

Henry had waited a year for this game. He had once more fought back from injury and was fit and raring to go for the final. The hard work, the lonely nights, the sacrifices were all for this 70 minutes of hurling.

Henry settled straight into it with the first point of the game from a free. Soon Kilkenny were five in front. Everything was going well. Henry was winning loads of ball but he wasted a few chances. He was kicking himself at half-time. But a goal from Michael Fennelly had them in front.

It was another clash of the Titans against Tipp. They just didn't know when to accept they were beaten. But Kilkenny drove on again with a great team performance. Richie Hogan added a second goal and they fought off Tipp in the closing stages to win by four points.

'Yes, Richie! What a game!' roared Henry.

He may not have been at his sparkling best. But that didn't take away from the joy. A year before he had stood in the same spot with tears in his eyes, defeated, injured and people saying his career was over. Now he was an All-Ireland champion once more. For a truly remarkable eighth time.

As he made his way off the pitch with the Liam McCarthy Cup in his hand, he had just one person he wanted to thank more than any other. Not the goal scorers, Richie and Michael, not Cody, not the physios or doctors. No, he made his way to hug the one person who had helped him more than any other during the dark times. Deirdre.

'We did it!' he said as they hugged with tears of joy in their eyes.

Chapter 19

The King vs the Prince

Henry was now considered the greatest hurler of all time. The undisputed king. But over in Galway they had a superstar of their own coming through. Joe Canning, a mega-talented young hurler from Portumna, was lighting up the game and starting to get plenty of attention. Henry saw for himself just how good Canning was in a club match between Ballyhale and Portumna. Young Joe was on fire that day and blew Ballyhale out of the water. He scored two goals and five points for Portumna, putting Henry in the shade. That game was the first of many battles they would have on the field. If Henry was the king, Joe was the prince. They were the two best hurlers of their generation.

After last year's win over Tipperary, Henry took some time off over the winter. He had surgery on a shoulder injury and missed most of the league. But he was back in action again for the start of the championship. He scored 10 points in their first game against Dublin. A big win and everything seemed well. But the mighty Cats would soon fall to a great upset. To Galway and Prince Joe in the Leinster final.

Not many people gave Galway a hope before the match. But Joe had other ideas. Right from the start he was unplayable. He caught a high ball over the head of Kilkenny's Jackie Tyrrell, turned quickly and blasted the ball home.

Goooooal! What a goal! Joe Canning!

It was still early, but Henry knew Kilkenny were in trouble already. Galway were immense from back to front. And Joe scored everything that moved. Henry could hardly get a touch. Cody was scratching his head on the sideline. At half-time Galway were miles ahead by 2-12 to 4 points.

Kilkenny weren't giving up that easily, though. Richie Hogan scored a goal. Then Henry had a chance when Galway's goalkeeper made a mistake.

Goooooal! Shefflin taps it into the empty net! Is the comeback on?!

But there was no way back for the Cats. Galway were the Leinster champions with a 10-point win. Joe Canning was the hero. He had scored a goal and 10 points.

It was a huge shock. But Kilkenny's season wasn't over yet. The loss to Galway was a wake-up call, so they did what they always did when things went wrong. They went back to the training pitch and worked harder than ever before.

Kilkenny bounced back with wins over Limerick and then Tipperary again. They were back in the All-Ireland final for the seventh year in a row. And who would they be up against? Galway and Joe. It was Henry's chance for revenge. He was going for his ninth All-Ireland title, to become the most decorated player in the history of the game. That made him nervous. But not as nervous as the thought of playing Galway again.

There was an electric atmosphere at Croke Park that day. It was Galway's first outing in the All-Ireland final in seven years. Their fans were beyond excited. Deep down below the stands in the dressing room, Cody was laying out the tactical plan.

'We were destroyed in the Leinster final. These lads are dangerous. Canning, Hayes and Burke are the danger men. We have to man mark them,' he said calmly.

Henry took it all in. No matter how many times he sat in the dressing room on All-Ireland final day, he always felt as nervous as the first day. This one felt like a bigger game than any other. The hand of history was on his shoulders. He was about to play the game of his life.

Galway made a fast start, as they had in the last game. Canning was causing trouble up front again.

Canning ... He's made a lot of ground ... Great touch ... Great vision ... Gooooal! How did he do that?!

Canning added more points to his goals. Galway were well in charge. But Henry was starting to motor. He scored three late frees to cut the gap at the break to just five points.

'We need more out the park. We're being overrun,' Cody barked in the dressing room. 'Henry, I want you to move out to centre-forward. Get on the ball. Make things happen.'

And that's exactly what Henry did. He revelled in his new freedom. He charged into everything that moved in a Galway jersey. He seemed to catch every ball. He hooked, blocked and ran his socks off. He felt completely in the zone. He was setting up his teammates and scoring at will himself. Kilkenny were right back in the match now. With minutes to go the referee blew his whistle.

A penalty to Kilkenny!

The scores were level. The game was in the balance. Henry thought long and hard about going for goal, but it was too risky. Instead he went for a point to put Kilkenny ahead. They were about to become All-Ireland champions again, all thanks to Henry's monumental second half display. But Joe had other ideas. Like Henry, he refused to accept defeat for his team. Galway were awarded a late, late free. It was the last puck of the game. Joe stepped up to take it.

This to level the match ... The pressure of the entire county of Galway on him.

It's over the bar! It's a draw! The match will go to a replay!

It was one of the most exciting games of hurling there had ever been. Joe was immense, Henry even better. In truth neither player deserved to lose. So they went back three weeks later to do it all again.

Henry picked up where he left off in the replay, once again influencing the game with his every touch. Galway again had the better start. Daithí Burke fired two goals inside a minute midway through the first half. It was set to be another classic. But Kilkenny turned up the heat and Galway finally fell away. Henry knocked over nine points and Walter Walsh came up with a man of the match performance on his first start for Kilkenny with a goal and three points. In the end, Kilkenny won out easily. Henry was an All-Ireland champion for the ninth time.

Amid the celebrations he found Joe. The pair simply nodded and shook hands, a sign of the respect the two great players had for each other. The Prince would have better times ahead. But today belonged to the King.

Chapter 20

Family

They say cats have nine lives. Henry, the King of the Cats, had nine All-Ireland medals. It was some career. Henry knew the end was closer than the beginning now. When the Liam McCarthy Cup was lifted into the sky he looked across to Deirdre in the stand. His medal collection was growing and so too was his family. Sadhbh now had a brother, Henry Michael, and a sister, Siún. They were all there to share in his big moment. He felt like the happiest man in Ireland.

He spent most of the winter injured again. He suffered a broken ankle in a club match, which needed surgery and a long period of recovery. But there was no early comeback this time. Come the summer, he still wasn't ready. His ankle was still swollen and he was way short of match practice. Kilkenny played Offaly without him. It was the first time he missed a championship match in more than 10 years. The end of a remarkable record. His teammates did the business without him, but they were stunned by Dublin in the next round. The defeat was a massive shock.

That meant Kilkenny had to go into the qualifiers, where they were up against old rivals Tipperary at Nowlan Park. Henry was itching to get back in action. The physio told him it was too soon, but Henry wasn't taking no for an answer. He told Cody he was ready and he was named on the bench.

For all the big days he had at Croke Park, this felt like a special occasion. It was an epic battle against the old enemy Tipp. The crowd cheered every puck, shoulder and score. The game was good enough to be an All-Ireland final. Henry came on for the last six minutes and set up a score. Kilkenny held on for a win that was celebrated long into the night.

Henry was still a long way from his best and still struggling for fitness. The next match against Waterford went to extra time. Henry was called ashore early, not something that happened often in his career. He was really struggling. Kilkenny managed to scrape through, but they were a shadow of the team that won the All-Ireland the summer before. Their miserable year was finally ended by Cork in the quarter-final. Typical, thought Henry. It would have to be them. That red jersey again.

To top off a year to forget, the referee took a dim view of a heavy hit from Henry.

Red card! Shefflin is sent off!

Henry was speechless. He knew it was a badly timed tackle. But no way was it a red. He just walked off the pitch with his head down. A fitting way to end a year to forget.

He wondered if he was past it.

'Maybe it's time to pack it in,' he said to Deirdre one night. 'I've had a good run.'

He knew some fans were already writing him off. They said that his body had taken too much punishment, that he'd never be back to his best after all the injuries. The pace of the game now was quicker than ever and the hits were harder. He was getting older too. The age gap between him and his opponents was getting wider. He questioned if he would be able to keep up.

His job was demanding, too. Maybe now was the time to stop playing hurling and spend more time with Deirdre and the kids. He asked himself if it was time to quit. For good.

But he knew the answer. Just 12 months earlier he had been named the best player in the whole country. He wasn't going to give up that easily. He still had more to give. He wasn't finished with Kilkenny hurling yet. No way! It was time to give it everything for one more year.

Chapter 21

Perfect 10

Henry wasn't going to let a red card against Cork be his final act in a Kilkenny jersey. He stayed injury-free over the winter for the first time in years. That meant he was fitter than ever coming back to training and he was even beating some of the younger players in sprints. It was a great feeling. The Kilkenny players talked a lot over the winter about what had gone wrong the year before. They were determined to win back the Liam McCarthy

Cup this year. For Henry, it meant more than for most. He knew it was his last year with the Cats and he wanted to go out in style.

Henry scored 12 points in their first league match, which was against Clare. Even though his team lost, it felt good to start the season on form. Next up, he was among the goals again as Kilkenny won a high-scoring game against Tipperary. He wasn't playing when the Cats beat Galway and Dublin but he was back again to face Waterford. He scored seven more points, but his performance was a bit below his usual standard, and he missed a few easy frees.

He paid the price the next day, when Cody named him on the bench. He had been the main man for so many years and now he was a substitute. It was a new feeling and he didn't like it. It reminded him of all those years ago when he was starting out, struggling to get on the school team at St Kieran's.

Henry and Deirdre's fourth child, Freddie, was born in April, which made things busy at home again. But it gave Henry a great pep in his step. He realised again that there was more to life than hurling.

Kilkenny's next game was a league semi-final against Galway. Henry came back into the starting team and he was right back on form. He scored four points from play and was named man of the match.

'You've still got it, Sheff! Even though you're an old man!' laughed Cha in the dressing room afterwards.

'I'd still give you a run for your money!' Henry laughed back.

The final against Tipperary went to extra time. Henry had a bad day and was taken off early. He was so disappointed. So often he had been the hero. Now, Cody felt he didn't even need him on the pitch when it mattered most. It was frustrating. One day he played great, and then the next day not so good. It's often the way it goes for sports stars when they get older. They can't be great in every game anymore. Kilkenny won the game, but Henry felt empty afterwards. He didn't know it at the time, but that was the last match he would start for Kilkenny.

Henry pushed himself harder than ever in training over the next few weeks. He was hoping to prove himself fit enough to get back onto the team. But he was stretching his body to breaking point and he damaged a bone in his foot again.

Owwwww!

Another spell on the sidelines. That meant he missed the first game of the championship against Offaly. Kilkenny played brilliantly and ran up a huge score. Henry watched on from the sidelines and knew in his heart that he had a long way back into the starting team.

Their next match was against Galway. Henry was back in full training now, but he was left out of the starting team.

'Henry, you're on the bench,' Cody told him bluntly. 'I need you to be strong mentally for us. We need your experience. The young lads look up to you. We'll need you to play a big part late on in games.'

Henry couldn't hide his disgust and said nothing. But he knew Cody was right. The team needed him and that was all that mattered. It wasn't just about himself. Every player has to do what they can to help the team.

Kilkenny were nine points up when Henry came on against Galway. But suddenly everything changed. Galway staged an amazing comeback and suddenly the Cats were behind. Henry moved out the field in search of ball hoping to make a difference. And then he got his chance ...

Shefflin! From an impossible angle! How did that go over?! An amazing point from the maestro!

The game finished in a draw. Henry was hoping he had done enough to be recalled to the starting team for the replay. But he was disappointed again. He came on for the last eight minutes and played his part again as Kilkenny won through.

They marched on to another Leinster title with victory over Dublin. Henry scored three points after coming on as a sub. He felt like he belonged again!

Next up was a win over Limerick in the All-Ireland semi-final. Henry played an important role in the closing stages again. He was starting to enjoy his new role as the senior man in the team, helping the younger players and coming on to use his experience in the closing stages.

Kilkenny reached another All-Ireland final, playing Tipperary yet again. It was a mad-cap, helter-skelter game. Kilkenny scored three goals but still couldn't find a way to beat Tipp. Henry came on for the last three minutes and could only look on in horror as Tipp scored three quick-fire points to level the game. Henry ran for his life and threw himself into every challenge, hoping for the one chance to be the hero. But it wasn't to be. The game ended in a draw. Yet another replay.

Henry took everything in on the bus journey to Croke Park for the replay. This was it. His last big day out for Kilkenny. He hadn't told anyone else yet, but inside he knew it. He wanted to remember it all. The colour and noise of the fans outside. The smells and sounds of the stadium. The flicks and flakes of a hurl in the heat of battle on the pitch. He was determined to enjoy every single second of it.

The game was a lot tighter than the first day. Still nothing between the sides. Henry made a rousing speech in the dressing room at half-time.

'You have this, lads. Tipp are on the ropes. Up the intensity and we'll win. Give it everything you've got!'

With 12 minutes to go, Cody looked across to Henry and gave him a nod.

'In you go, Henry!'

This was it. Henry's last act. Twelve minutes to make his mark.

The crowd gave a huge roar when Henry appeared. It gave Kilkenny a lift. And seconds later, they took control of the game.

Goooooal! Richie Power hits the net. Has he won it for the Cats?!

'Yes, Richie!' roared Henry. 'Keep the heads now, lads. Keep running!'

A few minutes later Henry found some space. He got his hand on the ball and slipped a perfect pass to Colin Fennelly to set up the final score of the game.

'Yesssss!' Henry pumped his fist. He knew they would win it now.

'What a ball, Sheff!' shouted Fennelly with a thumbs-up.

The referee blew the whistle and the game was over. Kilkenny were the champions. Henry had played his part and entered the record books.

He hugged his teammates and jumped for joy on the pitch. He high-fived the fans and waved and blew kisses to his family and friends. He shared a moment with Cody. A big hug. The final act of the greatest player–manager combo in the game. Together, they had achieved it all.

Henry slowly climbed the steps of the stand to lift the Liam McCarthy Cup for the last time.

He raised it into the air to the biggest cheer of all from the Kilkenny crowd. They knew they'd never see the likes of Henry again.

A perfect 10 All-Irelands. More than any other player in the history of the game. Henry the great.

Chapter 22

End of the Road

Henry had one last piece of business to tend to before he finally stepped off the hurling pitch for good. He wanted one last shot at glory with Ballyhale.

Just a few weeks after his last match for Kilkenny, he was togging out once more for a clash with Danesfort in the Kilkenny championship. Henry showed no signs of slowing down with age. He scored six points from play in a big win for Ballyhale. He loved being back playing for the parish again without the pressure. He felt like he was a little boy, playing simply for the love of the game. He scored another three points in the next game against St Martin's to set up a county final against Clara.

It was a huge occasion at Nowlan Park. More than 8,000 fans packed in for what many thought might be their last chance to see the great Henry Shefflin on the field. As it turned out, it wasn't his finest game in the green and white jersey. But his teammate TJ Reid came to the rescue with 10 points in a superb performance to make Ballyhale county champions again.

'Some game, TJ! Well played!' laughed Henry as he slapped TJ on the back.

'I learned from the master!' said TJ, smiling from ear to ear.

Henry was now the old head on the team and it gave him great joy to see the younger players like TJ keeping the traditions of Ballyhale hurling alive. It was a great night in the village.

But they didn't have long to celebrate. The following Sunday they were off to Dublin to play Kilmacud in a Leinster semi-final.

TJ was on fire again, scoring another goal and eight points. Henry had a fine game too, scoring a goal and two points himself as Ballyhale marched on.

The deadly duo continued where they left off in the Leinster final against Kilcormac/Killoughey from Offaly. They were a super team, with the two giants Pete and Ger Healion at the heart of their play and they gave Ballyhale an almighty fright, taking the game to extra time. Henry showed all his class and experience to pull the strings for Ballyhale and see them over the line. He scored four points from play, and TJ knocked over an impressive 10 points. Ballyhale were Leinster champions again. Henry was now just two games from glory once more. What better way to end his career, he thought, than one last big day at Croke Park.

Henry played another fine game in the semi-final against Galway side Gort. He was playing without a care in the world, running injury-free and roaming the pitch hunting scores, smashing over points from all angles. Ballyhale gobbled up Gort and were into the All-Ireland final. Limerick side Kilmallock were the opposition for what would be Henry's last ever appearance on the hurling field. It was only ever going to end one way.

Henry was emotional before the game. He knew every inch of Croke Park, and had been here for so many big days. This was different, though. He promised himself he would enjoy it, but he was finding it hard to fight a feeling of sadness.

He went through his usual routine on a big day, knowing each moment would be the last. The bus journey to the stadium, the cheering crowds, driving under the tunnel into the stadium, and entering the dressing room, pulling up his socks, lacing his boots, slipping on the jersey, and picking up his hurl. And the last pre-match task, giving a rousing speech in the dressing room.

'Lads, I've won everything in the game. But this is the most important match in my life. I'm not losing my last match,' he said with a crack in his voice.

'Come on, lads!' the other players roared together. 'Do it for Henry!'

They tore into Kilmallock, firing point after point. Midway through the half, Henry made his mark. He latched on to a long puckout and flicked it into the path of Colin Fennelly ...

Shefflin sets up Fennelly! What a strike!

Ballyhale were much the better side and had the game won long before the end. That gave Henry time to take in every moment. What a way to finish up. Sailing to victory in an All-Ireland final with his hometown team. His brother Paul on the pitch, his old school mates Aylward and Cummins beside him, along with new stars TJ Reid and Colin Fennelly.

The referee blew the whistle, calling time not only on the match but on Henry's career. He raised his arms in the air and took a deep breath. He had done it.

Here he was, standing in the middle of the pitch in Croke Park, with his friends and family from home watching on. The band of brothers from Ballyhale. He had a huge hug with Cummins and Aylward. It seemed like only yesterday when they were young boys celebrating at the Lisdowney Sevens. Now they were at the end of the journey. Older and wiser, but still sharing the same passion for hurling and for the parish.

Henry took a moment to himself as he slowly made his way back to the dressing room. His dream had come true.

***

A few weeks later, when all the hype had died down, Henry and Deirdre decided to take the kids for a spin. It was a fine spring day and so they decided to head for one of Henry's favourite spots. The beach in Tramore, a short drive south into Waterford.

They all jumped out of the car with excitement when they got there. Henry grabbed a few hurls and sliotars out of the boot of the car. He never travelled too far without them. The sand was soft and golden and seemed to go on as far as the eye could see. Huge waves were rolling in and crashing on the shore.

'Here, Dad! Catch!' shouted Henry Michael as he flicked a sliotar towards Henry.

Henry caught it on the end of his hurl, ran a few steps and handpassed it to Sadhbh.

'Nice catch!' he said as she took the ball, gently jogging over the sand in her bare feet.

'Here, Mam!' she said, launching the ball high into the blue sky. 'Catch that!'

Deirdre ran a few steps towards the edge of the sea and jumped to catch the sliotar. But as she landed, she stumbled and splashed right into the water.

'Aghhhhh! It's freeeeezing!' she roared.

Henry and the children burst out laughing. Even little Siún and baby Freddie let out a giggle from the comfort of their buggy.

Henry took a deep breath and let the fresh sea air fill his lungs. He was in his happy place.

He thought back over his life. His childhood, running round the squash court behind the house, wearing a helmet and jersey that were way too big for him. The advice from his mam and dad, Henry and Mai. The family puck abouts as he learned from his brothers Tommy, John and Paul and his sisters Aileen, Helena and Cecilia. His mam driving him to matches, sometimes getting lost on the way. The long days on Friary Field. His first ever real match with the school in St Patrick's, with Mr Dunphy roaring from the sideline.

And then when he was a bit older, his struggles in the entrance exam and difficult years at St Kieran's. The day he broke out of hospital to watch Kilkenny at Croke Park. His first steps with the Kilkenny minors and under-21s. The craic in his college years in Waterford. All the injuries, pain and criticism.

And the good days too. He'd had more than most people do.

Ten All-Irelands with Kilkenny. Thirteen Leinster championships. Six national hurling leagues. Eleven All Stars and three Player of the Year awards. And to cap it all, a third All-Ireland club title with his beloved Ballyhale. It was the perfect way to end a glittering career.

He looked over to the water and his family splashing about in the sea. He smiled at Deirdre and his beautiful children: Sadhbh, Henry Michael, Siún and Freddie. He didn't know it then, but baby Tom would soon make it five. Everything he ever dreamed of had come true.

A tear came to his eye as he thought back on it all. He realised he never hurled for himself. He did it all for them.